YOUR
BODY

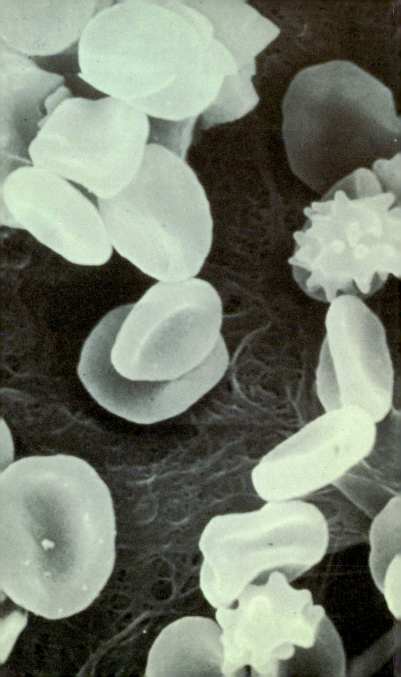

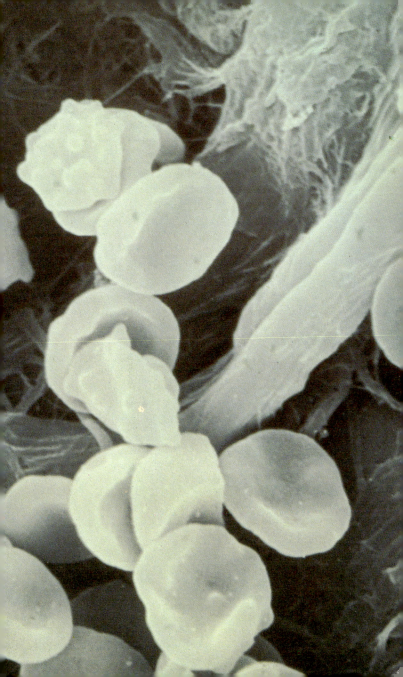

Contents

YOUR BODY

By
Steve Parker

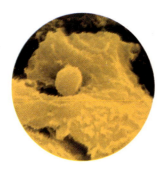

Editor: Deri Warren
Designer: Ben White

Piccolo
A Piper Book

The Human Machine

Think of any complicated machine, such as the Space Shuttle, an oil rig or a nuclear power station. These are marvels of modern technology, but how do they measure up to the following extraordinary machine?

This machine has an internal framework of girders, plates and panels which are strong but light, to support and protect its various parts. It has powerful winch-like devices that can move any part of the machine, in any direction. It has **sensors** that detect temperature, moisture, light, sound and touch. Every part of the machine is linked by thousands of miles of communication cable to a control centre which is unimaginably more complicated than even the most sophisticated aircraft cockpit.

The machine can find and take in its own fuel. It is able to build and repair itself. In

Left: Androids (human-like robots) are a science-fiction fantasy. In reality, no machine is nearly as sophisticated and complex as the human body.

fact, when it is fully constructed it can make new versions of itself. The amazing mystery machine is, of course, the human body.

The body machine even invents and builds other machines to help it. Machines like hydraulic diggers and word processors can increase our strength, speed and thinking abilities, but none of them could exist without us. We build them, fuel them, repair them, and replace the parts that wear out. Yet our bodies can do all these things for themselves, and even do most of them automatically without us having to think about it. This leaves our minds free for less machine-like, more 'human' activities such as talking, inventing, painting pictures or just daydreaming.

Systems, organs and tissues

The day-to-day running of the human body is carried out by its various **systems**. For example, the nervous system (brain and nerves) carries messages from one part to another and generally co-ordinates the whole body. The urinary system (kidneys and bladder) filters the blood to remove wastes and excess water.

If we look at each body system in turn we see it consists of several parts, called **organs**. The circulatory system, for example, is made up of the heart, arteries, veins, and other blood vessels, as well as the blood itself. An organ usually has one important job to do. The heart pumps the blood, the kidney filters wastes from the blood, and so on.

The closer we look, the more intricate the body becomes. Each organ is made up of several kinds of **tissue** such as nerve tissue, muscle tissue and bone tissue. Under a microscope, a piece of one of these tissues is seen to be formed from thousands of building blocks – each one the same, like bricks in a wall. These building blocks are called **cells**.

Building with cells

The cell is the basic unit of all living things, and the

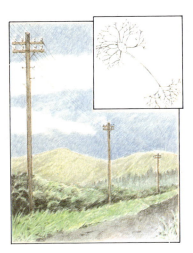 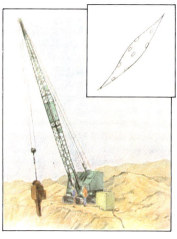

Each of the cells that make up the body are designed for certain jobs. The nerve cell (above) carries electrical signals to the brain along its thin strands, like messages going along phone wires.

The muscle cell (above) is long and thin, but shortens to give the body its pulling power. Machines such as cranes and winches use a similar principle to move their loads.

human body is no exception. The microscopic animal called the amoeba consists of only one cell, whereas a human body has 50 million million cells (that's 10,000 times the number of people in the world). The average cell is about 30 microns (one-thirtieth of a millimetre) across, though there are dozens of different shapes and sizes of cells.

The particular design of a cell depends on the job it does. Our cells are specialized to carry out their particular job very well, but they need looking after. They need supplies of oxygen, energy and nutrients. They also require a warm, watery environment. Each cell does its own job but it also depends on many others doing theirs.

In this book we'll see how these cells are assembled into tissues, how different tissues make up organs, how organs combine into systems, and how the systems work together to make the amazing human machine.

Cells called osteocytes (above) have long 'fingers' that reach into bone tissue to keep it healthy. In the same way, we use scaffolding to reach all parts of a building for construction and repair.

The liver cell (above) changes nutrients and other substances into forms that the body can use – rather like a kitchen food-processor perparing food for cooking by chopping and blending it.

The Body's Computer

Comparing the human brain to a computer can help us to understand how the brain works. A computer uses a 'language' of tiny electrical currents which travel along wires and through switches. The same thing happens in the brain but the 'wires' are nerve cells, or **neurones**.

Both receive, sort, store and recall information. Depending on its program a computer, like a brain, can add, subtract and make logical decisions such as the next move in a chess game. And both are in control – the brain controls the body, while computers are in charge of other machines such as TV screens, printers or robot car-makers.

In some ways a computer is more reliable than a brain. In theory, a computer never forgets, has an unlimited memory, and recalls information almost at once and exactly as it was stored.

Learning is the key

A human brain can give the square root of 4 in a fraction of a second, but only because it recognizes this sum from previous experience and remembers the answer. It would take much longer to calculate the square root of

A computer could probably beat most of the world's chess players (below). But it is not capable of emotion, wit or humour, or able to appreciate beautiful music or art (above).

5. A computer can answer both these sums correctly in a few thousandths of a second, but it does the calculations from scratch every time. And here is the vital difference – the computer does not learn from experience.

A computer is not what we would call 'intelligent'. It can't really understand, or imagine, or have ideas, or create beautiful pictures or music. It is limited to what its programs tell it to do. Even advanced computers have an I.Q. (intelligence quotient) estimated at only 0.2; the average brain has an I.Q. of 100.

What sets the human brain apart from a computer is its ability to understand, reason, learn and adapt. Using information brought to it from the body's senses, the brain continually reprograms itself as it assesses situations, decides on actions and learns from the results. The rest of the human body is not particularly outstanding compared to other animals which are stronger, faster and have better sight or hearing or have sharper teeth or more powerful jaws. But our brains are superior, and are the reason for our success.

Decisions, Decisions

Every minute of every day, the brain receives far more information than you would find in the biggest encyclopedia. Sights, sounds, smells and tastes are only a few of the sensations received from the outside world. More messages arrive from the thousands of sensors inside the body, telling the brain about the levels of oxygen in the blood, or whether the bladder is full. It is the brain's job to collect, analyse and filter the mountains of information so that our conscious mind can cope.

processes such as heartbeat and breathing, but in an automatic fashion so that we don't have to think about them.

On the 'middle' level the brain sorts through incoming information and picks out anything which, from past experience, it considers might be important. (For example, among other street noises you may pick out the squeal of tyres on the road outside, which could mean an accident.) This information passes to the 'higher' level, the conscious mind. It

Three-level system

In simple terms, the brain operates on three levels. The 'lower' level controls vital

1: Detect. Paul's ears pick up all sounds and send the information to his brain's hearing centres.

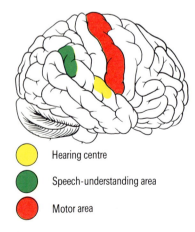

Hearing centre

Speech-understanding area

Motor area

is here that we become aware, decide what to do, and then act.

The cortex

All this filtering and decision-making takes place in the surface layers of the two large hemispheres which make up the bulk of the brain. The layers are called the **cerebral cortex**. Certain areas of the cortex deal with information coming from certain parts of the body. These areas are termed **centres**.

For example, the hearing centres are on each side of the cortex. The ears detect sounds and convert them to electrical impulses, which travel along nerves to the hearing centres.

Once information is received and processed, it is used for decision-making. Having made its decision, the brain needs to tell the body to act. It organizes this from the part of the cortex called the **motor area**. The motor area sends signals along nerves to the muscles, which move the body.

The entire process of detecting, deciding and reacting sounds complicated, but when you are crossing the road and a car suddenly comes round the corner, you can do it in a split second.

2: Decide. If an overheard sound is important (such as Paul's name) it is brought to his conscious attention.

3: React. Paul's motor area tells his neck muscles to turn his head towards the source of the sound.

Making Connections

One morning a friend phones to say that school is closed for the day, due to burst plumbing. You think about this, decide to throw a party, and phone some friends to invite them over.

Your nerves make it possible for you to carry out your brain's decision – just as the telephone wires fetch and carry information. No phone, no party.

In's and out's

There are two kinds of nerves. **Sensory** nerves bring information from the sense organs to the brain. **Motor** nerves take instructions from the brain to the muscles. Together the brain and nerves make up the nervous system.

Like other body systems, the nervous system is built from cells. The basic nerve cell is called the neurone. There are an estimated 10,000 million neurones in the brain, and around 15,000 million in the rest of the body.

The neurone is specialized to transmit the tiny electric impulses that make up a nerve message. The impulses travel from the cell body along a thin, wire-like strand called the **axon**. Axons are very long, while the neurone's body is of normal cell size. In a neurone running from the base of the spinal cord to the foot, a single axon may be over a metre long – but only a hundredth of a millimetre in diameter.

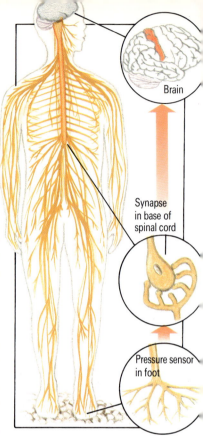

Brain

Synapse
in base of
spinal cord

Pressure sensor
in foot

14

When you tread on a sharp stone, nerve messages flash from the foot to the brain in a split second. This distance may well be over a metre, yet only a few neurones (nerve cells) are involved along the way. One carries the message from the foot to the base of the spinal cord, another carries it up the cord to the base of the brain.

The sharp, stabbing pain is carried by fast nerves with thick axons. They are covered with a sheath of fatty substance called myelin, which helps to speed conduction. Fast nerves transmit impulses at over 120 metres each second.

The dull, aching sensation is carried along slow nerves with thin, naked axons. They carry information which does not have to get to the brain at once. Their impulses travel at the speed of only a metre or two each second.

Fast and slow

Not all nerves transmit impulses at the same speed. When you stub your toe, for example, there is an initial sharp, stabbing pain, then a second or so later the dull ache comes through. This is because these two sensations travel along different types of neurone, which carry the impulses at different speeds.

Bridging the gap

When the electric impulse reaches the end of an axon it has to jump a gap, called the **synapse**, to reach the next neurone. The impulse makes the end of the axon release a chemical which flows across the gap and starts a new impulse on the other side, in the next neurone.

In reaction to a sharp stone, nerve messages flash to the leg muscles (telling them to lift the leg) and also to the face and throat muscles, which grimace and exclaim.

The impulse is received by a thin, drawn-out part of the next neurone, called a **dendrite**. Dendrites are much shorter than axons. Most neurones have only one axon, but a dozen or more dendrites.

The entire system is so complicated because it has so many interconnections. In the brain, one neurone might connect with up to 50,000 others, and impulses are passed to only a selection of these, depending on the circumstances. This is like a telephone switchboard sending calls around an office building. The nature of the incoming call determines where it's put through to. Similarly, if a message from the eyes comes through to the brain, it travels along different paths than a message coming from the ears.

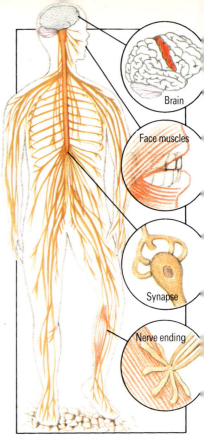

Brain

Face muscles

Synapse

Nerve ending

Putting your foot down
Walking on a pebbly beach is an awkward business. When you put your foot down, pressure sensors in the skin of the sole are stimulated and send out a stream of nerve impulses. Each impulse is about the same strength, but the harder the sensors are squashed, the faster they produce them. A highly stimulated sensor can send out 1,000 impulses each second.

The impulses flash along the axons of sensory neurones, up the leg to the spinal cord. The cord is a massive bundle of neurones between

continue to walk across the pebbles, the motor part of the nervous system is put into gear. Impulses are sent from the motor area of the cortex, back down the cord, across synapses, to the leg muscles.

At the end of the last motor axon is a special type of synapse junction which connects to the muscle. When the nerve impulse arrives it releases chemicals, which cross the gap and set off the muscle contraction which lifts the foot.

But many other things are happening as well. The brain is organizing and co-ordinating hundreds of other muscles to keep the body balanced, such as moving the arms and shifting weight from one side to another. If the stone is particularly uncomfortable, messages go to the breathing muscles and the vocal cords, telling them to say 'Ouch!' (This is an automatic reaction which may have come about as a means of warning other people of possible danger, or attracting their attention and help.) The face muscles grimace. If the sensation in the foot is actually painful, though, the brain can be bypassed altogether – how this happens is explained on the next page.

the body and the brain. The impulses cross synapses and continue up the cord to the brain, where they are shared out among the neurones in the cerebral cortex. It is only now that you 'feel' the uncomfortable pebbles.

Making a move
Once the brain has decided that the body should still

Acting on Impulse

When you touch a newborn baby's cheek, it turns to the side of the touch. If you carefully let a baby fall backwards just a little, it is startled and throws out its arms and legs, and grabs with its hands. These actions, each one happening automatically in reply to a certain signal, are called **reflexes**.

A new baby's brain has had very little experience on which to base its behaviour. So to help a baby through the first days and weeks, it is born ready-equipped with various reflexes. For example, the 'rooting' reflex, when it turns towards a touch on the cheek, helps it to find the nipple for breast-feeding.

The new baby, with its jerky and unco-ordinated movements, is like a bundle of reflexes. But it soon learns to control most of these, and its actions become smoother and more purposeful.

Bypassing the brain

A reflex is automatic because once the signal is received, it is not fed straight to the conscious part of the brain. For example, if you cross your legs and tap your leg just below the kneecap, your leg will jerk up. The signal comes from sensors in the

Left: The gripping reflex is one of the new baby's automatic actions. It will hold on tightly to anything placed in its hand.

tendon below the kneecap. Sensory neurones carry the nerve impulses to the spinal cord, where they connect to motor neurones. These take the impulses back to the leg muscles, which contract and jerk the knee.

In the meantime, impulses also travel from the sensory neurones up the spinal cord to the brain. So the brain is told about the signal, even though it can do nothing to stop the response.

The adult brain has learned to control some reflexes, such as emptying the bladder when it holds a certain volume of urine. But the body still needs many other reflexes. For example, the pupil of the eye automatically widens as light levels fall, to let in enough light to see by.

The body usually relies on reflexes in situations where there is only one possible response (such as widening the eye pupil) or where there is no time to wait for the brain. If your finger touches something dangerously hot, a valuable split-second could be lost while the nerve impulse travels up to the brain, which then has to make a decision and send a message back to remove the fingers from the heat source. A reflex is more direct, faster, and does not rely on a brain whose attention might be elsewhere.

In dim light, the pupil of the eye is wide open, to let in as much light as possible.

In bright light, a reflex makes the pupil smaller so the eye is not dazzled by too much light.

Memories

Suppose you need to make a telephone call and you don't know the number. You look it up in the directory and then repeat it to yourself, perhaps out loud, as you dial. But unless it's an important number and you make a real effort to remember it, you will have forgotten it after a few minutes.

How long are memories?

There are several types of memory. To remember the telephone number above you used 'short-term' memory which can last up to half an hour or so.

There is also a very limited 'working' memory. This is used, for example, to remember what you have just been saying so that you can finish the sentence. If this memory is preoccupied with something else, you can find yourself stopping mid-sentence, having forgotten what you were going to say.

At the other end of the scale is the 'long-term' memory which can last almost a lifetime. The brain is very choosy about what it puts into its long-term memory. It tends to transfer only the information it thinks might come in useful in the future. For example, if a telephone number is important enough the brain copies it from the short-term to the long-term memory.

Storing the past

Compared to any computer the human brain has an incredible capacity for storing information and then recalling it. Not only phone numbers, facts and figures, but a lifetime of sights, sounds, smells, words, the basics of language, behaviour patterns and much more are crammed into a lump of nerve tissue one-and-a-half litres in volume and one-and-a-half kilograms in weight.

Sweet dreams

Each night the body takes a rest, but the brain never

Below: The human brain has an amazing ability to store information, even in comparison with a library of computer disks or books.

stops. Electrical recordings of the brain's activity during sleep have shown that there is still plenty going on. Sleeping may be a time for the brain to sort through the day's events, discarding some memories and programming others into the main memory banks.

There are two main kinds of sleep, REM and non-REM. During REM sleep your eyes

Very young children sleep for more than half the day, but the average adult spends only about a third of his or her life asleep.

move quickly to and fro beneath closed eyelids (REM means 'Rapid Eye Movement'). During non-REM sleep your eye muscles, like many other muscles in the body, are relaxed.

Using Your Senses

Close your eyes. Point upwards with each hand, and then slowly bring your forefingers together so that their tips touch.

How did you manage this? Our senses provide information about the outside world – but you could not see your fingers, or hear them, or smell, taste or touch them before they came together.

However, our senses also provide information about the 'inside world' – inside the body. Stretch sensors in the muscles and joints of the shoulders and arms send messages to the brain, telling it the position of each arm and hand. This is how you know where your fingers are.

Such sensors are all over the body. They make up the **kinaesthetic** sense, one of several we have in addition to sight, hearing, smell, taste and touch.

The sensitive body

The human body is remarkably sensitive to its surroundings. In the front of the head are the eyes – two sophisticated cameras, linked together for 3-D vision. In the sides of the head are the ears – sensitive microphones with sensors for positioning and moving the head. Below the cameras is the nose – an odour sensor, for detecting molecules in the air; below this, in the mouth, is another for detecting molecules in food and drink. And all over the body surface are sensors for touch, pressure, temperature difference and pain.

Above: Even when flying through the air on two wheels, our sense of balance tells us whether we are heading for a safe landing or not.

22

Sense organs are extensions of the nervous system. Each sensor is a nerve cell specialized to collect information about what is happening in the world outside the body, such as rapid changes in air pressure (a sound wave), and then send nerve impulses to the brain.

Our sense organs, though sophisticated, are only detectors. The eye cannot 'see' – it simply detects light rays of different colours and intensities. It is only when the nerve signals are analysed by the brain that we see.

All eyes and ears
In its everyday life the human body relies mainly on sight and hearing. If vision fails, other senses sharpen to compensate – or, rather, it is the brain that sharpens. A blind person's ears pick up the same sounds as a sighted person's but the blind person's brain is more experienced at listening. It picks out all the tiny details which a sighted person would miss, being too busy with vision to listen this carefully.

Right: Sometimes we choose to concentrate on only one sense at a time. Even a tricky job like tying shoelaces can be done by touch alone, while eyes and ears are occupied.

SIGHT

HEARING

SMELL

TASTE

TOUCH

Windows on the World

Vision is our most precious sense. Eyes keep us in touch with the world – but at a distance. Thanks to our eyes, we can see danger long before it is close enough to do damage. Sight so overpowers the other senses that people tend to shut their eyes, for example, when they want to concentrate on music. It is estimated that four-fifths of everything the brain knows has come through the eyes.

Every image of our world, from a mountain landscape to these words, is detected by two layers of specialized nerve cells, each layer the size of a postage stamp. They are the **retinas**, which line the rear three-quarters of the inside of each eyeball.

The retinas measure light intensity and colour and send coded nerve impulses along the two optic nerves to the visual centres at the back of the brain. Here they are analysed for shape, pattern, motion and all the other features of the colour, 3-D

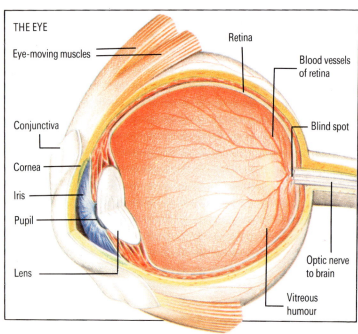

THE EYE

Eye-moving muscles

Retina

Blood vessels of retina

Conjunctiva

Blind spot

Cornea

Iris

Pupil

Lens

Optic nerve to brain

Vitreous humour

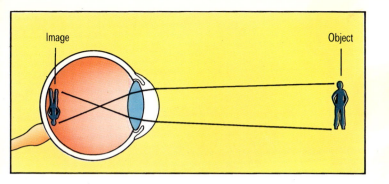

moving pictures we see in our mind's eye.

Seeing in dots

Like a picture printed in a newspaper or book, we see the world as a pattern of tiny dots. A full-page picture in a book, covering about 600 square centimetres, contains around eight million dots (you can see them with a magnifier). A retina, measuring only six square centimetres, has over 130 million 'dots'. Each 'dot' is a light-sensitive cell that detects a ray of light and turns it into a nerve impulse.

But before an image reaches the retina its brightness and focus must be adjusted. Brightness is controlled by the iris, a disc of muscle tissue at the front of the eye. It is about 12 millimetres in diameter and has a hole in the middle called the pupil. The bigger the pupil, the

Above: The image on the retina is upside down, but the brain turns it over so that we see things the right way up.

more light enters the eye, and so the brighter the image. The pupil automatically enlarges from a minimum of one millimetre in bright light, to over eight millimetres in dim light, under control of a nerve reflex (see page 19). The iris also contains **pigment** cells which give our eyes their colour.

Staying in focus

Three parts of the eye carry out the job of focusing. The cornea, the clear dome just in front of the iris, provides about three-quarters of the eye's focusing power. Just behind the iris is the lens, which provides most of the other quarter. Third is the vitreous humour, the clear

25

jelly that fills the inside of the eye and keeps it ball-shaped.

The lens is adjustable, to give clear vision at different distances. When the eye looks at something near, the ring of muscle around the lens contracts and becomes smaller. The lens, suspended inside it, becomes fatter due to its natural elasticity. A fat lens has more focusing power to deal with diverging light rays from a nearby object.

When the eye's gaze switches to something far away the muscular ring relaxes and enlarges, and the lens is pulled thinner. Its focusing power is reduced to cope with almost-parallel light rays

Above: Judging distance: looking at nearby objects makes you 'cross-eyed'. Detectors in the eye muscles tell the brain that the eyes are looking inwards, so the brain knows that the object is very close.

from a distant object. As we scan a scene the lenses are continually changing shape so that they always throw clear, sharp images on to the retinas.

Rods and cones

Packed into the retina are nerve cells specialized to turn light energy into nerve impulses. There are two main cell types, **rods** and **cones**. The 130 million rods detect

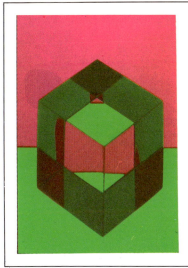

only light intensity and so see in black, white and shades of grey. They can work in very poor light. The seven million cones pick up colour and fine detail, but they work only in bright light.

Inside the rod and cone cells are chemicals called **visual pigments**. When light falls on the cell it breaks down the visual pigment and this fires off a nerve impulse. The pigment is then quickly rebuilt, ready to detect another ray of light. The rods and cones then send, via other nerve cells in the retina, the basic information of vision along the optic nerve to the brain.

Above: One cube – but each eye sees a slightly different view. With the book 30cms away, stare at both pictures (hold your hand side-on between them, to help each eye see only one picture). The cube 'jumps' into 3-D.

Seeing in 3-D
The brain assembles two images, one from each eye, and combines them into one 3-D image using a variety of clues. For example, each eye sees a slightly different view of an object in the foreground, and the object is in front of a slightly different part of the background. Near objects overlap faraway ones.

The brain recognizes perspective: faraway railway

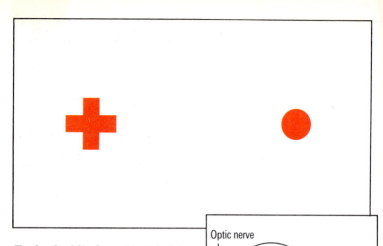

To do the blind spot test hold the page 40cms away. Close your left eye and stare with your right eye at the cross. As you move the page closer the red spot on the edge of your vision disappears when its image falls on the blind spot.

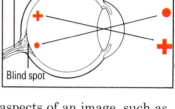

Optic nerve

Blind spot

lines appear to be closer together than those in the foreground. It also uses 'parallax'; that is, as the head moves from side to side, near objects seem to move across the distant ones.

Seeing is believing?

Although a new baby's eyes work as well as an adult's, it has to learn to 'see'. When it is born, its brain is suddenly swamped with unfamiliar visual information which it must learn to interpret. The visual centres in the brain learn to respond to certain aspects of an image, such as horizontal or vertical lines.

If an image is not complete, or not quite as expected, the brain tends to fill in the gaps. On top of the rods and cones in the retina are neurones and tiny blood vessels. Depending on the angle of the incoming light rays, some rods and cones are in 'shadow' areas beneath the neurones and vessels, and so they are not stimulated. At a very early age the brain learns to fill in these gaps so that we always see a complete picture.

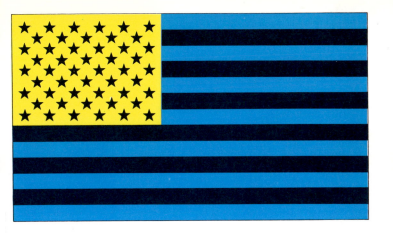

Colours are also not what they seem. When we see an unfamiliar colour we tend to change it in our mind so that it fits in with the colours we already know. When we are shown a range of similar colours again, we pick out not the original shade but a more familiar one. Some people cannot distinguish certain colours. Blue and green, for example, may look the same, while all other colours look normal. We call this 'colour blindness'.

As the brain learns to interpret what the eyes record, it invents various rules and short-cuts. We end up seeing what we think or expect to be there.

Right: All our senses are capable of being tricked. Is this a rabbit, or a duck?

Above: Stare at the flag for 20 seconds, then quickly look at a white area to see an 'after-image' of the flag in different colours. This is because the cone cells which see the flag's colours become 'worn out' for a few seconds, so the eye cannot see the full range of colours that make up white light. The missing colours make white look like blue and red.

Hearing and Balance

Any sound engineer knows that the more times you transfer a recording from one tape to another, the poorer the quality of the sound becomes. With each transfer the sound becomes duller and muddier.

So, it is surprising to learn that in the ear there are at least seven or eight different transfers. Yet this organ can detect the slightest drop in the quality of sound from the best hi-fi equipment.

Banging the drums

The ear detects the vibrations of air molecules which form sound waves. The vibrating molecules funnel into the ear canal and hit the eardrum at the end, making it vibrate. The eardrum, which is about nine millimetres across, is in contact with a tiny bone, the hammer. This is connected to another tiny bone, the anvil. This is attached in turn to the stirrup. These three bones are the smallest in the body.

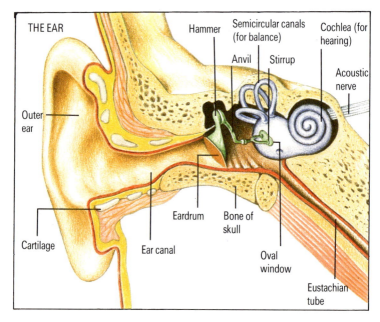

THE EAR

Hammer

Semicircular canals (for balance)

Cochlea (for hearing)

Anvil   Stirrup

Acoustic nerve

Outer ear

Eardrum   Bone of skull

Cartilage   Ear canal

Oval window

Eustachian tube

Vibrations pass along the bones and from the stirrup they are transferred to another drum-like membrane, the oval window. Behind this is a fluid-filled chamber called the **cochlea**. The oval window passes vibrations into the fluid.

The cochlea is a pea-sized, snail-shaped organ embedded in the skull bone behind the eyeball. Vibrations in the fluid within it shake microscopic hairs which grow from cells on a long membrane inside the cochlea. The hair cells are specialized nerve endings, and when their hairs vibrate this starts nerve impulses which travel along the acoustic nerve to the brain.

There are about 20,000 hair cells in each cochlea, and each one has up to 100 hairs. Low-pitched sounds cause the long membrane and hairs to vibrate in a certain way, while high notes cause a different type of vibration. The brain deciphers the vibrations – and so we hear.

A microphone, which converts sound waves via a moving magnet or crystal directly into electricity, is fairly simple by comparison.

Left: Inside the ear. The Eustachian tube connects to the back of the throat and allows air into the middle ear. This equalizes the air pressure on each side of the eardrum so that it moves freely.

Below: A hare can swivel its large ears to pick up faint sounds and pinpoint where they are coming from. Humans do not have this ability, though a few of us can waggle our ears.

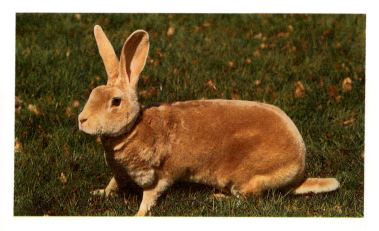

Turning down the volume

Like any self-respecting hi-fi the ear has a volume control, to cope with the rustle of leaves one minute and the roar of traffic the next.

The volume control is in three parts. One is a tiny muscle which tightens to stiffen the eardrum so that it does not vibrate so easily. A second muscle restrains the three tiny bones so that they, too, vibrate less freely. Both muscles contract under the control of a nerve reflex, a fraction of a second after the ear hears a very loud noise.

Thirdly, very loud sounds alter the angle of contact between the stirrup and the oval window so that vibrations are passed on less efficiently.

Loudness is measured in decibels (dB). A volume of 90 dB may damage the ear; anything louder than this certainly does. The sound at some discos and rock concerts is over 100 dB, and exposure to it night after night can damage hearing permanently.

Trained ear

When we say a musician has a trained ear we really mean a 'trained brain'. Unless there is some disease or disorder present, most of

Above: Sound waves from the radio reach the left ear (1) only one hundred-thousandth of a second before the right ear (2). But the brain detects this tiny time difference and knows this means that the radio is to the left of the head.

us hear roughly the same sounds. Differences arise in how experienced the brain is in listening.

However, the ear does become less sensitive as we grow older. Babies and children can hear higher-pitched sounds, such as dog whistles and a bat's squeaking, than older people. This is because the hair cells in the cochlea lose their hairs and the eardrum may stiffen and become less responsive as it ages.

Balancing act

If you bang your head or spin round too fast, you feel dizzy.

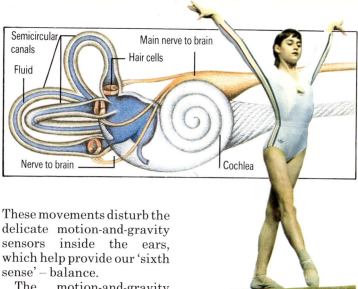

Semicircular canals

Fluid

Main nerve to brain

Hair cells

Nerve to brain

Cochlea

These movements disturb the delicate motion-and-gravity sensors inside the ears, which help provide our 'sixth sense' – balance.

The motion-and-gravity sensors are next to the cochlea inside each ear. Three tiny curved fluid-filled tubes, called the semicircular canals, are set at right angles to each other. Head movements cause currents in the fluid, which stimulate nerve cells in the tubes' lining to send more impulses to the brain.

Near where the tubes join there are more hair cells with tiny crystals on the tip of each hair. These act as microscopic weights, that always pull the hair tips downwards. This tells the brain about the position of the head in relation to the pull of gravity.

The brain collects all this information and analyses the

Above: We have three tiny fluid-filled tubes called semicircular canals in each ear. These detect gravity and head movements, so that with practice we can balance even on a narrow beam.

angle of the head, in which direction it's moving, and how fast. It combines this with information from the eyes, the kinaesthetic sensors in muscles and joints, and the pressure sensors (particularly on the soles of the feet). As a result the two-legged human design, so difficult to copy as a machine, can not only walk on flat ground but can also balance on a tightrope.

Skin Deep

Have you ever wondered what house dust is? Part of the 'dust' in any home is the family's dead skin. Every day the body loses up to one gram of skin. Dead flakes are rubbed from its surface by washing, drying, brushing hair, handling objects, and the pressures of sitting and lying.

So that the skin does not wear through, like an old carpet, the rubbed-off portions are continually replaced by cells dividing rapidly just below the surface. In fact just below its dead outer layer, skin is very much alive.

Millions of skin sensors tell the brain about touch, pressure, temperature and, if necessary, pain. Tiny blood vessels expand or contract to help control body temperature. Three million sweat glands produce sweat to cool down the body if it gets too hot. Sebaceous glands make the oily substance called sebum, which keeps the skin and hair waterproof and supple. Skin is certainly not just a lifeless bag for our insides – it's a complex, active and extremely sensitive organ.

Skin structure

Skin has two basic layers. The **epidermis** makes up the top half-a-millimetre or so, though on areas like the soles of the feet this layer can be up to five millimetres thick.

Dividing cells at the base of the epidermis produce new cells which are slowly pushed towards the surface in a conveyor-belt process as more cells form beneath. As they move to the surface the cells flatten, fill with a hard substance called **keratin**, and die.

Above: For a blind person reading Braille, touch replaces sight. The sensitive skin on the fingertips feels the patterns of tiny raised dots that make letters and numbers, plus a few simple words.

When they reach the surface the dead skin cells form a strong interlocking barrier, like tiles on a roof. This flexible covering is ideal for repelling germs and water.

Under the epidermis is the **dermis**, which is about two millimetres thick. Here live most of the sensory cells, as well as glands, hairs, nerves and blood vessels.

Below: The outer two or three millimetres of the body are packed with sensors of many kinds, detecting everything from the lightest touch to crushing pain.

Under the dermis is a layer of fat, which is thicker in some people than in others. Fat tissue helps keep heat in and cold out, and it acts as a shock-absorber to cushion internal body organs.

The whole skin covers an area of nearly two square metres and weighs three kilograms. It is the body's largest organ, and receives nearly one-third of the blood pumped out by the heart.

Sensors in the skin
Tying shoelaces with your eyes closed is fairly easy, and

THE SKIN

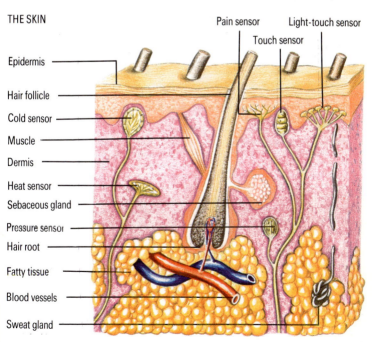

Pain sensor Light-touch sensor
Touch sensor

Epidermis
Hair follicle
Cold sensor
Muscle
Dermis
Heat sensor
Sebaceous gland
Pressure sensor
Hair root
Fatty tissue
Blood vessels
Sweat gland

you can do it almost auto-matically. This shows our remarkable sense of touch – how quickly the brain can process the sensory nerve impulses from the fingers, and how deftly the muscles of the hands can manipulate the laces.

The sensory nerve endings in the skin come in various shapes and sizes and are positioned at different depths. These different de-signs detect touch, light pressure, heavy pressure, pain and temperature dif-ferences.

Certain parts of the body can detect touch sensation better than others. For ex-ample, on the skin of the back, pinpricks must be about two centimetres apart before the brain registers two separate points. But in the fingertips, touch sensors are so close together that they can detect pinpricks only two millimetres apart.

Our skin sensors show what biologists call habi-tuation. When you first put on your clothes in the morn-ing, you can feel them against your skin. After a few minutes this feeling has gone – unless you move. This is because the touch sensors fire nerve impulses rapidly at first, when you dress, but

under continued stimulation they fire less and less, or become 'habituated'. When clothes rub suddenly they fire again. So the sensors respond more to changes in stimulation rather than the level of stimulation.

Gripping stuff

Car tyres are made to hold the road even in wet and slippery conditions. Our fin-gers have a similar high-grip design, in the ridges that make up our fingerprints. Every person ever tested has proved to have a unique fingerprint, which is why they are used as evidence when catching criminals.

The skin on the fingers and hands continually produces small amounts of sweat to aid in gripping. Wash your hands and dry them thor-oughly, then quickly try to pick up a pin. You will find

Above: Hair which is not cared for by regular brushing and washing will fray and split – as shown in this photograph taken down a microscope.

Below: Hair type depends partly on the shape of the follicle it grows from. Straight hairs come from circular follicles (1), wavy hairs from oval ones (2), and curly hairs from rectangular ones (3).

that it's much easier when the fingers are slightly damp from a thin film of sweat.

At the tips of our fingers are the nails, which are made of dead, keratin-filled cells. The only living parts are the roots. A nail grows about two millimetres each month, though fingernails grow faster than toenails. Nails act as a hard base for the sensitive skin of the fingertips and toetips to press against, so they may help our sensitivity to touch.

Hairy humans

The bodies of our prehistoric ancestors were covered in long fur. We now use clothes and central heating to stay warm. Nevertheless we still have tiny hairs all over our bodies, except the palms and soles, and we have 'fur' on our heads and other places. This 'fur' is still important in

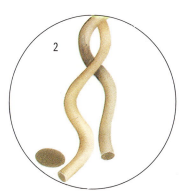

Left: In cold conditions, the skin's blood vessels become narrow so less heat is lost at the surface. 'Goose pimples' help to trap the warm air around hair follicles. **Below:** In hot weather, blood vessels widen and sweat evaporates to keep you cool.

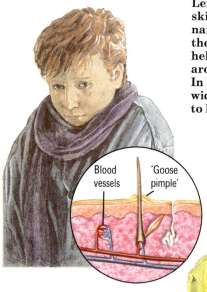

Blood vessels

'Goose pimple'

Heat escapes

Sweat

keeping the body warm. A new baby, with very thin hair, loses up to a third of its body heat from its head.

There are 100,000 hairs on the average head. Each grows from a pit in the skin called a follicle. A hair lengthens on average by one centimetre a month, and lives for three years before being pushed out by a new hair growing beneath. A hundred hairs fall out daily.

The hair shaft is dead and senseless, but sensory endings wrapped around its root detect the slightest movement. When we feel the wind blowing against our skin, it is actually because the wind is moving the tiny hairs growing there.

Glowing with health

Do clean skin and a well-balanced diet really make a person 'glow with health'? To an extent, yes.

Someone who eats very unhealthy food, lacking in vitamins and other substances, can suffer from brittle, cracked and sore-looking skin. Hair becomes dull and lifeless. It is not true that an occasional bar of chocolate gives you spots. Spots are more likely to be due to poor washing, except during the teenage years when they are largely a part of growing up.

Colour is skin-deep

Skin colour comes from pigments, chiefly **melanin**, produced in special skin cells called melanocytes. In the epidermis about one cell in ten is a melanocyte. If a person has active melanocytes they make a lot of pigment and the skin is dark. If the melanocytes are inactive the skin is light. If there are a few active melanocytes scattered here and there the skin has freckles.

One thing that stimulates melanocytes is sunlight. Sunlight also helps the skin to make vitamin D, which the body needs for healthy bones and teeth.

In sunny places, the melanocytes become more active and make more melanin. The result is a suntan. The extra pigment protects tissues in the dermis from the sun's damaging ultraviolet rays, although the epidermis can become dry, wrinkled, and at risk from skin cancer.

Groups of people who have lived in sunny places for many generations have developed dark skin as protection against sun damage. But the colour is only skin-deep. Underneath we are all much the same.

Below: The dark skin of a suntan helps protect the tissues beneath from the Sun's harmful rays.

On the Move

Every move you make, every breath you take, every single heartbeat, chewing what you eat – every physical activity of the human body involves the muscles. Without muscles, the body would be still and lifeless. And without the bones, which provide a rigid internal framework, the body would collapse like a heap of jelly.

As usual, without the brain as controller and co-ordinator of the whole system, nothing would happen. The brain sends out messages along motor nerves, which work the muscles, which pull the bones, which move the body.

Levers and limbs

Archimedes, the famous mathematician of ancient Greece, was supposed to have said: 'Give me a lever long enough and I will move the world'. Given an arm or leg long enough and strong enough you could do the same, because the limbs are designed like levers. Bones in the arms and legs form a strong, rigid framework. Muscles provide the pulling power and are attached to the bones near their joints.

For example, the muscles in the upper arm are attached just below the elbow to the upper part of the forearm (see page 48). This arrangement means the muscles have to shorten only a small amount in order to move the other end of the lever (the hand) a long distance.

However, although muscles can pull, they can't push. So one muscle is needed to move the lever one way, and another to move it back again. This means that about half the body's muscles are relaxed at any one time. It has been estimated that if all the muscles in the body could pull in one direction at the same time, they could lift some 25 tonnes – but only over a distance of a few centimetres. With the body designed as it is, a super-heavy weightlifter can manage to raise about one-quarter of a tonne above his head.

Left: It is unlikely that nature intended us to develop our muscles to this extent. When we move we need flexibility and stamina as well as strength.

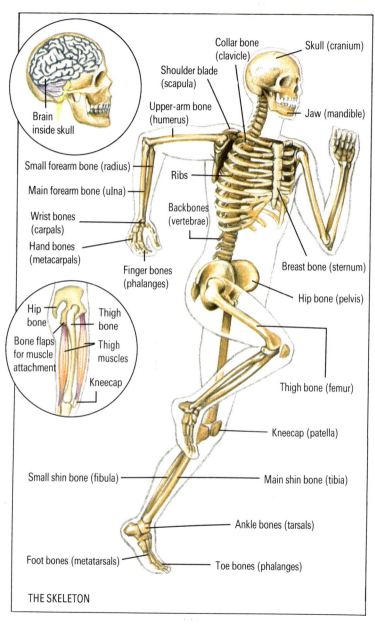

Brain
inside skull

Collar bone
(clavicle)

Skull (cranium)

Shoulder blade
(scapula)

Jaw (mandible)

Upper-arm bone
(humerus)

Small forearm bone (radius)

Ribs

Main forearm bone (ulna)

Backbones
(vertebrae)

Wrist bones
(carpals)

Hand bones
(metacarpals)

Finger bones
(phalanges)

Breast bone (sternum)

Hip bone (pelvis)

Hip
bone

Thigh
bone

Bone flaps
for muscle
attachment

Thigh
muscles

Kneecap

Thigh bone (femur)

Kneecap (patella)

Small shin bone (fibula)

Main shin bone (tibia)

Ankle bones (tarsals)

Foot bones (metatarsals)

Toe bones (phalanges)

THE SKELETON

Building with Bones

Since you were born, over a hundred bones have disappeared from your body. A baby has about 350 individual bones, whereas an adult has 206. But the missing bones do not dissolve away. As the skeleton grows and matures many of its smaller, separate bones gradually join together to make fewer, larger bones. A baby's skull, for instance, is made of several separate bony plates. As the baby grows the separate bones fuse together into one rigid 'brainbox'.

Changes like this show that bones are not the dry, brittle things we see in museum cases. Bones are very much alive and involved in many body processes, in addition to being the levers, cages, plates and boxes that form the body's internal framework.

Building with bones

Bone tissue has the construction engineer's favourite features – great strength coupled with light weight. In tensile (pulling) strength, bone is only slightly weaker than cast iron – yet is one-third its weight.

Bone has one great advantage over other building materials – it is alive. If a bone breaks, it mends itself. If the body's activities put strains on certain bones, these bones strengthen themselves where the stress is greatest.

If the body has fewer strains, though, bones tend to weaken. Calcium, one of the minerals that gives bone its hardness, is gradually dissolved away from the bones, since they do not need to be so strong. The early astronauts, weightless in their spacecraft, lost calcium from their bones and their skeletons weakened. Back on Earth and under the pull of gravity, the bones regained their calcium and

Left: The thigh bone is connected to the hip bone . . . and so on throughout the skeleton. Besides being the body's rigid framework, bones have other jobs. The skull or 'brainbox' forms a hard case to protect the delicate brain (top circle). The hip bone has large flaps to anchor the powerful thigh muscles that we use for walking and jumping (bottom circle).

their strength. Astronauts now do special exercises in space to keep their bones and bodies healthy.

Bones as anchors

The body's muscles need to pull on something, usually a bone. Many bones have broad flaps and plates providing a large surface area, which gives very firm anchorage for strong muscles. The shoulder blade (scapula) anchors several muscles which work as a team to move your arm in any direction you wish.

Bones as protectors

Some bones help to protect softer organs. The bowl-shaped hip bone (pelvis) shields the bladder, intestines and other organs, while backbones and ribs form a flexible cage around the heart and lungs. The backbones have holes inside them, forming one long tunnel in which the delicate spinal cord is cushioned from knocks and twists.

Bones as blood makers

In a child, most bones are hollow and contain a soft, jelly-like material called **marrow**. The marrow makes billions of red cells for the blood. To distribute these

Below: Bone tissue shows up as white or light grey on an X-ray. Here a bone has broken and will gradually repair itself. A blood clot forms at the break, then bone-making cells produce new bone to glue the ends together. The process takes several weeks.

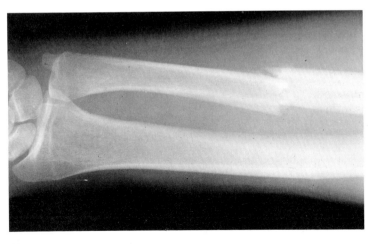

cells, bones have a rich supply of arteries and veins. In an adult, blood cells are only made in the marrow of the skull, breast bone, backbones, hip bone and some limb bones.

People suffering from certain types of leukaemia, a cancer-like disease of the blood cells, may have a 'bone marrow transplant'. The surgeon injects a donor's healthy bone marrow into the sufferer's bones, in the hope that it will replace the diseased marrow and start making healthy blood cells.

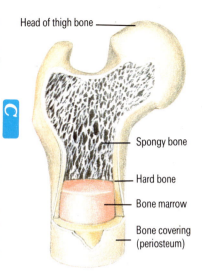

Head of thigh bone

Spongy bone

Hard bone

Bone marrow

Bone covering (periosteum)

A mineral store

A living bone is about one-third water. It also contains a lot of calcium, potassium and phosphorus, which form a crystal-based material that gives bone its hardness and strength. These minerals are also used in many other processes, such as sending nerve messages that make us move. If the food we eat lacks minerals, then the body can use the stores from its bones for more urgent needs. This weakens the bones, but prevents the nerves from becoming paralyzed.

The bare bones

The biggest bones are the two femurs (thigh bones),

Above: Bones are not solid. They are more like tubes, combining strength with lightness. The hard outer layer of the thigh bone surrounds light spongy bone and marrow in the centre.

which make up over a quarter of the body's height. The smallest bone, only three millimetres long, is the stirrup inside the ear. The skull is formed by about 20 separate bones fusing together during growth.

There are 26 separate backbones making up the spine, and 12 pairs of ribs. Each arm has 32 bones, each leg 31. Over half the body's bones are found in the hands and feet.

Human Joinery

Modern animated models, like the strange creatures in space films, can be amazingly realistic. But despite the hi-tech model-making and special effects, we can usually tell when a creature has machinery inside it. Somehow its movements are not quite as easy and supple as those of real, live animals. These smooth movements are helped by the joints which connect the various bones of the body.

Jobs for joints

Like the joints in any machine, the 200 or so joints of the human body have different designs for different jobs. Not all joint designs allow movement – some are like the glued-together joints used in carpentry. The edge of one bone is 'glued' to the edge of another with tough connective tissue, which means the joint is extremely strong but immoveable. The bones of the face are joined in this way.

However, other joints do permit movement. Hinges, swivels, ball-and-sockets and other designs all allow movement in certain directions, without the bones separating or 'dislocating'.

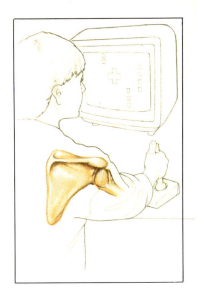

The shoulder joint is a ball-and-socket design, similar to a computer joystick.

In general the strongest joints are those which allow very little movement, such as those between the bones in the foot. In a really flexible joint that moves in almost any direction, like the shoulder, there is less strength and stability, and more risk of dislocation.

Inside a joint

In a mobile joint the two bone ends are covered by a tough, smooth, shiny substance called **cartilage**.

To lower friction even further, the cartilage-coated

46

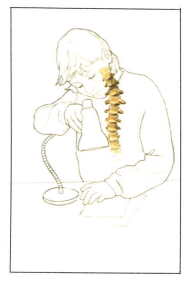

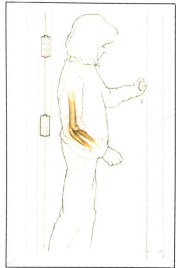

The spine has many small joints giving overall flexibility, like a desk lamp.

The elbow is a hinge joint, resembling the hinge that opens a door.

bone ends hardly ever touch. They are separated by a thin film of slippery fluid which acts like the oil that lubricates the moving parts of a car's engine. But unlike cars, humans do not need a regular oil change. The fluid is continually made and absorbed by the 'synovial capsule', a thin bag which encloses the joint.

Around the synovial capsule are strong, slightly stretchy belts called **ligaments**. Each end of a ligament is glued by connective tissue to each bone of the joint. The ligaments, plus the various muscles that work the joint, provide stability and limit the range of movement so that the bones do not dislocate easily.

The joints between the backbones are unusual. There is a separate pad or 'disc' of cartilage between each pair of bones. As you walk about during the day these 20-odd discs are squashed by the weight of the upper body. So in the evening you are about a centimetre shorter than when you woke up that morning.

Pulling Power

The runner is on the last lap of the race, well ahead of her rivals, when suddenly she is struck by cramp. Her calf muscles tighten painfully, and she hobbles off the track to stretch and massage them back to normal.

Most of the time we take our muscles for granted. We can move parts of the body any way we wish, quickly or slowly. We can pick up heavy things, or precisely manipulate small objects such as a needle and thread. We only really notice our muscles when they go out of control, as in cramp, or if we work them too hard and they become weak and trembly. From the body's bulkiest muscle, the gluteus maximus of the buttock, to the smallest, the one-millimetre-long stapedius in the ear, every move we make depends on our muscles.

Levels of control
There are about 650 voluntary muscles in the body. They are called 'voluntary' because we can make them pull when we want them to. Most voluntary muscles move the skeleton and so shift the body.

Above: Cramp is a painful, uncontrollable muscle contraction. Its causes include chemical upsets in the muscle due to a lack of salt or a build-up of wastes.

Right: Roadies and others who regularly carry heavy loads need good lifting technique: feet slightly apart, knees bent and back kept straight.

Muscles that move the body, such as the biceps and triceps, work as partners. One shortens to

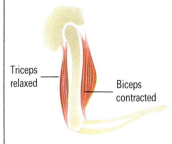

1

Triceps relaxed

Biceps contracted

Left: Over a hundred different face muscles helped to give the *Mona Lisa* her fascinating smile.

pull the forearm up (1), then relaxes as its partner shortens to move the forearm down (2).

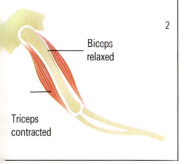

2

Biceps relaxed

Triceps contracted

But the voluntary muscles are not under individual control. The brain tends to organize them into teams. When the brain orders: 'Raise the left hand', not only the three or four arm-raising muscles contract. Muscles in the shoulder, torso and legs adjust the body's balance and posture.

We learn many movement patterns in early childhood and they become almost automatic. They are controlled mainly by the cerebellum – the lower, rear part of the brain. The cerebellum co-ordinates the nerve messages going out to muscles so that, with practice, complicated movements become smooth and easy. When we learn to play the piano or serve at tennis, we realize just how many muscles need controlling.

There are plenty of other, 'involuntary' muscles in the body. They drive breathing, heartbeat, digestion and many other essential processes. They work automatically, without the need for conscious instructions from the brain.

How a muscle contracts

Like other body organs, a voluntary muscle is made of cells. Muscle cells, called muscle fibres, are the super-giants of the cell world. Each fibre is one-hundredth of a millimetre in diameter but 30 or 40 millimetres long when relaxed. Its speciality is shortening to almost half its relaxed length when stimulated by a nerve impulse.

Each end of a voluntary muscle tapers into a strong, rope-like tendon which is usually anchored to a bone. When the muscle shortens it moves one bone in relation to the other. And so the body moves.

Above: The graceful movements of the ballerina. Years of practice are needed to achieve such perfect muscle control.

Fuelling the machine

The muscles that move the skeleton can make the human body perform amazing feats. Top athletes run at over 30 kilometres per hour and hurl themselves over bars two metres high. Yet each of us has the same number of muscles, and the same number of muscle fibres. The difference is the size of each fibre. The more you use a muscle the bigger each fibre becomes, and this makes the muscle stronger.

Fuel for the muscles is oxygen and sugar (glucose), brought by the blood. An active muscle needs 15 or 20 times as much blood as it does when resting. To supply this the heart pumps faster and harder and the arteries to the muscles widen during exercise. The human body is about as fuel-efficient as a car. Twenty-five per cent of the fuel (food energy) is converted into useful work.

Busy means healthy

Evolution has designed the human body for an active life, gathering food and escaping from danger. Biologically we are not suited to lounging in armchairs and switching TV channels by remote control. If muscles are not used regularly they waste away, and this in turn affects many other parts of the body. Wasted muscles need less blood so the heart takes it easy. Being muscle itself, it also wastes away. Oxygen demand falls, too, so the lungs and breathing muscles become lazy. A body with wasted muscles, a weak heart and lazy lungs is almost asking for illness.

The remedy is simple. Use your muscles regularly, and make your body work hard. Stay active and be healthier.

Below: Jogging is good for you because the large leg muscles need lots of oxygen and energy, which keeps heart and lungs fit.

Take a Deep Breath...

Every few seconds from birth to death you take the breath of life – over 500 million breaths altogether in an average lifetime. We breathe air because our body cells need a supply of the oxygen it contains. Oxygen is a vital part of the chemical reaction which releases the energy that powers the cell's activities. If cells cannot get oxygen, they run out of energy and die. So the body must maintain a continuous supply of oxygen, from air in the lungs via the blood circulation, to all cells.

The brain is particularly sensitive to lack of oxygen. If breathing stops and the oxygen supply fails, within three or four minutes brain tissue has started to die.

Added extras

Getting oxygen into the blood, and removing the poisonous waste substance carbon dioxide from the blood, are the chief tasks of

the respiratory system. This system consists of the nose, throat, windpipe, lungs and chest muscles.

However, besides obtaining oxygen and removing carbon dioxide, the system has other functions. For example, it provides us with our unique method of communication, speech. It allows us to shout, sing, whistle, laugh and cry, grunt and groan. A yawn can convey tiredness, and a sigh can be tinged with sadness. We also use it for smelling: the pleasing fragrance of a rose or the warning smell of burning is carried on the incoming airstream.

The system also has its annoyances. Sudden, uncontrolled jerky movements of the diaphragm (the large breathing muscle under the lungs) causes an irritating attack of hiccups. But it also has many uses. Coughs clear the lungs and windpipe of dust and other particles breathed in, while sneezes and sniffs help to get rid of excess fluid produced by an illness like a cold.

Left: Divers cannot breathe oxygen dissolved in water. They need a Self Contained Underwater Breathing Apparatus – Scuba for short.

53

In, Out...

At rest we breathe about 15 to 18 times each minute. During activity our muscles use up more oxygen, and so we breathe faster and deeper to increase the air flowing through the lungs. After running a fast race the body's need for air takes over the mind and all we can think about is gasping for the next breath.

Control of breathing

As well as a means of taking in oxygen, breathing also gets rid of carbon dioxide. Carbon dioxide is a waste product from our energy-using chemistry, which will poison the body if it is allowed to build up. In fact it is mainly the level of carbon dioxide, not oxygen, in the blood that controls breathing rate and depth.

Sensory nerves in the 'breathing centre' at the base

BREATHING IN   BREATHING OUT

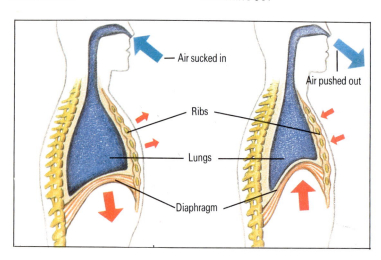

Air sucked in

Air pushed out

Ribs

Lungs

Diaphragm

To breathe in, the diaphragm contracts and flattens while the rib muscles raise the chest. The lungs are stretched larger and they suck air in through the nose and down the windpipe.

When you breathe out, your rib and diaphragm muscles relax. The elastic lungs, which had been stretched, spring back to their natural smaller shape and force air out again.

of the brain continually check blood flowing past them for carbon dioxide content. As soon as the level rises, the centre orders the breathing muscles to work harder and faster, and the excess carbon dioxide is breathed out from the lungs into the air.

Other sensors in some of the main arteries help with control of breathing. They respond to falling levels of oxygen in the blood as well as rises in carbon dioxide. They feed this information to the brain, and so supply a fine-tuning system. And because the reflex to gasp for air is stronger than the will, no one could willingly hold his breath long enough to suffocate and die.

Air conditioning
It's better for your lungs if you breathe in through your nose rather than your mouth. The nose is an air filter, moisturiser and heater, and so the lungs get clean, damp, warm air – just how they like it best.

Hairs in the nose trap floating dust, and sticky mucus on the lining picks up other particles. Water evaporates from the mucus to moisten incoming air so that it does not dry out the small

Below: The water vapour in breathed-out air condenses into droplets on a cold day. We lose half a litre of water daily like this.

airways and alveoli in the lungs. Without their thin covering film of water, the alveoli could not absorb the oxygen.

Blood in vessels just under the nasal lining gives up its heat to warm the air. These blood vessels break easily if you bang your nose, which is why nosebleeds are so common.

Inside the lungs
Each time you breathe in, your expanding lungs suck about half a litre of air down your throat and through

your windpipe (trachea). The windpipe is about 11 centimetres long and one and a half centimetres in diameter, and at its bottom end it splits into two tubes called bronchi. One bronchus leads to the left lung, the other to the right lung. These airways split over and over again, making more than twenty divisions altogether. By now the airways (called bronchioles) are less than a millimetre in diameter and still getting smaller. They end in bunches of tiny bubbles called **alveoli**, where the vital business of absorbing oxygen into the body occurs.

Clearing the lungs

To protect the alveoli the bigger airways have a dust-removing mechanism to trap any floating particles that get past the nose. There are special cells that make a sticky mucus which lines the airway and traps any dust. There are also cells coated with tiny hairs, called cilia, that constantly wave to and fro. The waving cilia push the mucus upwards in a continuous stream moving about one centimetre each minute. When enough mucus reaches the top of the windpipe we cough, and swallow it as phlegm.

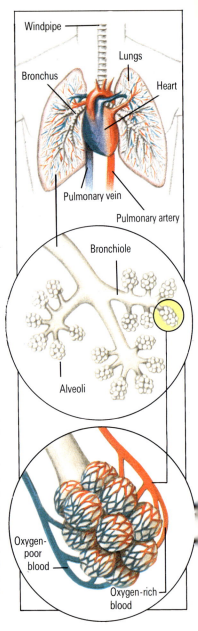

Windpipe

Lungs

Bronchus

Heart

Pulmonary vein

Pulmonary artery

Bronchiole

Alveoli

Oxygen-poor blood

Oxygen-rich blood

When the lungs are diseased, as in bronchitis, more mucus is produced and the sufferer has to cough more. And cigarette smoke kills the cilia-bearing cells, which is why smokers have so much trouble clearing their lungs.

Anyone for tennis?

In theory you could play a game of tennis on a pair of lungs. Between them the lungs have 700 million alveoli. Flattened out, all the alveoli would cover a tennis court. This is the huge area each of us has for absorbing oxygen and getting rid of carbon dioxide. Because the lungs are full of these air-filled microscopic bubbles they can hold two or three litres of air but weigh only one kilogram.

Each alveolus has a wall less than one-thousandth of a millimetre thick. On the outside of the wall are tiny blood vessels called **capillaries**. The blood, having been pumped along **pulmonary** arteries from the heart,

is 'stale' – i.e. low in oxygen. Fresh oxygen passes easily through the alveolar wall into the blood, changing it from dark to light red. It then flows out of the lungs and back to the heart along pulmonary veins.

While oxygen passes from air to blood, carbon dioxide passes from blood to air. The air you breathe in contains 21 per cent oxygen and 0.03 per cent carbon dioxide. When it comes out it has 4 per cent carbon dioxide and 16 per cent oxygen. This is still enough oxygen for another breath or two, which is why you can revive someone with the 'kiss of life' by blowing your own breath into their lungs.

Right: Super-heroes don't smoke. Cigarette smoke damages the lungs, makes you ill and shortens your life by putting you at increased risk from heart disease, bronchitis and cancer.

Speech

Many animals communicate by gestures and noises. But speech is quite unique to humans. Only humans have thousands of words and the vocal equipment to say them. And only humans have the brain power to combine them in millions of different ways, so that we say what we mean with great expressiveness, and understand what we hear with precision.

Below: Several parts of the mouth help to form sounds. The cavity inside the nose is also important – try speaking while holding your nose!

Dogs can be trained to respond to simple commands, and researchers have even taught chimpanzees to communicate with humans. But the chimps 'talk' in sign language. Their voice-boxes are just not designed for speaking our words.

Cords and reeds
You can talk while breathing in, but it's quite difficult. You can even make noises with your lips closed and your nose pinched shut, but only by moving air from your lungs up to your mouth and then back again. Like the vibrating reed in a woodwind instrument, the vocal cords which make all our spoken

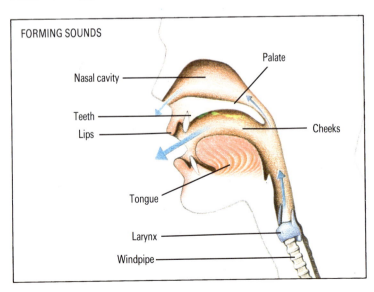

FORMING SOUNDS

Nasal cavity

Palate

Teeth

Lips

Cheeks

Tongue

Larynx

Windpipe

sounds work best when they are in a fast-flowing, one-way airstream.

The vocal cords are two folds of tissue, each about 15 millimetres long, inside the voice-box, or larynx, in the lower throat. Protecting the front of the larynx is a lumpy piece of cartilage. This is much more obvious in men than in women and we call it the 'Adam's apple'.

Normally the muscles connected to the cords are relaxed, so the cords themselves are loose and make no noise as we breathe. When the muscles in the larynx contract they stretch the cords taut, and when the lungs push air over the tight cords they vibrate to produce sounds. As the muscles pull harder the cords become longer and tighter and the sounds they make are more high-pitched.

Above left: Tongue, teeth and lips combine to make the sound 'th'. Above right: The lips are pushed out to make a hole for the sound 'oo'.

Shaping sounds

If you could place a microphone near someone's vocal cords, the sounds heard would be monotonous and surprisingly quiet. These basic sounds are given their shape (i.e. changing *eeee* to *oooo* or *aaaa*) by moving the cheeks, lips, jaw and tongue. The cavity in the nose also helps to shape sounds, as do the air-filled holes called sinuses in the skull bones.

The nose and sinuses resonate, like the hollow body of an acoustic guitar, to increase the voice's volume. When the nose and sinuses are blocked during a cold, we often have difficulty in pronouncing certain sounds.

The Body Pump

Many complicated machines depend on liquid circulated by a pump, and the body is no exception. Its cells depend on blood and on the heart to pump the blood. Blood brings oxygen and nutrients to every cell in the body, and takes away carbon dioxide and other wastes. Stagnant blood is no good – cells continually need fresh supplies. So the blood goes round and round, propelled by that marvel of engineering, the heart.

Romance and reality

For centuries the heart has been a symbol of love, affection, courage and other emotions. Hearts can be stolen or broken; they skip, race, leap and jump into our mouths. For encouragement we take heart, and for compassion we have a heart. Brave people are lion-hearted.

We now know that the heart is really only a blood pump, though a very sophisticated one. The real centre of emotions and feelings is the brain. It is the brain that orders the heart to pound as we take fright or flutter as we fall in love.

Two pumps in one

In fact the heart is made up of two pumps, side by side. The left pump sends blood around the body and back to the right pump, which sends it to the lungs and then back to the left pump. So the blood circulates in a figure-8 fashion, with the heart at the crossover.

Clench your fist and put it on your breastbone, two centimetres to the left of your midline (the line down the middle of your body). Just beneath your fist, your

fist-sized heart is pumping about once every second, for every minute of the day. In an average lifetime a heart beats 3,000 million times.

When the body is at rest, every heartbeat squeezes 60 millilitres of blood from each of the two pumps. During exercise the heart pumps up to three times every second, sending out 200 millilitres of blood from each side with every beat.

'I love you with all my heart'
. . . the body's pump is still a symbol of emotions, even though scientific evidence shows that emotions are based in the brain.

Inside the heart

The heart is nearly all muscle. It is a special type, called cardiac muscle, that never tires – unlike the voluntary muscles that move the limbs. Each side of the heart is a pump consisting of two muscle-bound chambers (see over). The upper chamber, the atrium, is small and slack-walled. It connects through a flap-like valve to a much bigger, thick-walled, muscular chamber called the ventricle.

The ventricle is where the pumping power comes from. When its muscular wall contracts it sends blood surging out of the heart and into the arteries at a speed of over 30 centimetres each second. When this happens the valve to the atrium snaps shut to prevent blood flowing back into the veins. If you put your ear to someone's chest you can hear the valves suddenly closing. They make the 'lub-dup' sound of a heartbeat.

The heart's blood supply

Although the heart has plenty of blood rushing through it, this blood is going too fast, and under too much pressure, to supply the heart muscle. Oxygen and food for the heart muscle is delivered by the heart's own blood

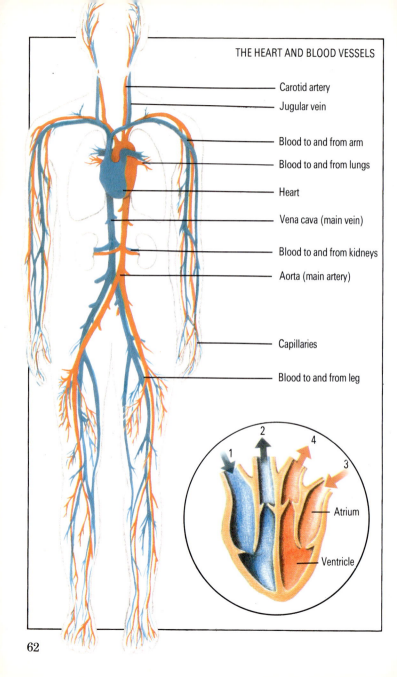

THE HEART AND BLOOD VESSELS

Carotid artery

Jugular vein

Blood to and from arm

Blood to and from lungs

Heart

Vena cava (main vein)

Blood to and from kidneys

Aorta (main artery)

Capillaries

Blood to and from leg

Atrium

Ventricle

supply. This consists of small arteries which come off the main artery, the aorta, from the left-sided pump. The arteries branch over the ventricles in the pattern of an elaborate crown, so they are called the **coronary** arteries (*corona* is the Latin word for crown).

In the way that the body depends on the heart for blood, so the heart depends on the coronary arteries. A heart needs lots of blood. It is less than one-hundredth of the body's weight but it uses up to one-tenth of the body's oxygen supply.

If the coronary arteries become blocked the heart muscle cannot get oxygen and so it starts to die. Unless emergency medical help is at hand the heart may stop. This is what we call a cardiac arrest or heart attack. If the heart stops, life stops. Coronary disease is one of the commonest killers today.

Left: Stale blood from body tissues enters the right atrium (1). It passes through a valve to the right ventricle, then out through another valve to the lungs (2). Recharged with oxygen it returns to the left atrium (3), through a valve into the left ventricle, and is then pumped out to body tissues (4).

Avoiding heart disease

You can do several things to lessen your chances of a heart attack. Take regular exercise, which makes the heart work hard and keeps it fit. Don't smoke. Don't eat too much fatty food, and don't become overweight. Medical research shows that some teenagers already have damaged coronary arteries, though the effects may not show until middle age. You are never too young to get into healthy habits.

The beat goes on

Heartbeat rate and volume are ultimately controlled by the brain. However, the brain controls the heart muscle not directly but through a pacemaker, a group of specialized nerve-like cells in the wall of the right atrium. The pacemaker starts a heartbeat. It sends a wave of electrical nerve impulses through the heart muscle to make it contract. (Electrical instruments can detect these impulses through the skin and scientists record them as an electrocardiogram or ECG.)

A heart on its own, out of the body, continues to beat because of its pacemaker. The atria contract about 140 times each minute, and the

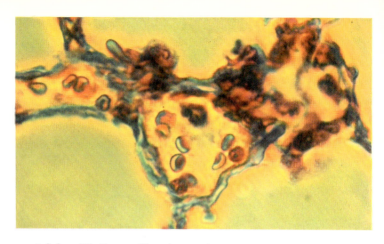

ventricles 30 times. But inside the body the pacemaker is under the control of the brain so it keeps to a resting rate of around 70 beats each minute. **Hormones** such as adrenaline also affect heart rate (see page 69).

Pulses of pressure
Blood leaves the heart along tubes called arteries. Their walls are thick and tough to withstand the surge of blood pressure that comes with each heartbeat. You can feel these pressure surges in the artery that runs through your wrist. We call it the pulse.

Not all arteries carry the bright red, oxygen-rich blood. The pulmonary arteries to the lungs contain dark red, low-oxygen blood on its way to collect more oxygen.

Above: This photomicrograph shows red blood cells inside a capillary. The walls of the capillary are made of flat cells, like curved paving stones, joined to make a tube. The walls are so thin that oxygen and nutrients can easily pass through them from the blood to the body cells beyond.

Where the action is
Arteries are simply blood transporters. They branch into every part of the body, dividing and becoming narrower. They eventually become the smallest blood vessels, capillaries, whose walls are only one cell thick. It is here that the real action takes place.

No cell in the body is very far from a capillary. Oxygen and nutrients pass easily through the thin capillary walls to supply the cells beyond, while waste substances travel from the cells into the blood and are carried away from the cells.

Its main job done, the blood flows back to the heart. Capillaries join, becoming larger and larger, until they form veins. These are thin-walled, baggy vessels that transport the blood back to the heart.

Valves and veins

Both the heart and veins have non-return valves that make sure blood flows only one way. You can see valves at work in your arm veins. Hang your arm down and choose a good, clear vein on the inside of your arm, midway between elbow and wrist. Press a finger on the vein, then squeeze upwards along the vein, to push the blood inside up the arm and back to the heart (1). There should be a place below which the vein remains empty (2). This is the site of a valve which is preventing the blood from returning back down the vein. If you remove your thumb, the vein should quickly refill upwards (3).

The lengths blood goes to

Heart, arteries, capillaries and veins form an enormous system. Joined together all the blood vessels in a single human body would stretch 100,000 kilometres – two and a half times round the Earth. Over 90 per cent of this length would be made up of capillaries.

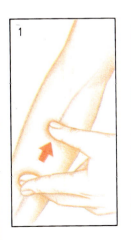

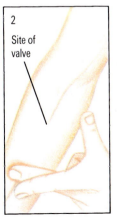

Site of valve

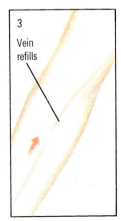

Vein refills

An All-Purpose Liquid

Most of us can endure the pain of a trodden-on toe or a bruised finger. We tend to be more distressed when accidents result in the sight of blood – even when there is little pain involved. Some people even faint at the sight of blood. Few things cause as much panic as the spillage of the body's life-fluid.

What is blood?
The average person has about five litres of blood. It is made of water, billions of cells, and hundreds of chemicals. The water and chemicals, without the cells, are called **plasma**.

Blood flows to every part of the body and provides the cells living there with everything they need. The blood flowing through our blood vessels provides a vital delivery and collection service for all cells in the body.

Fetching and carrying
All cells need oxygen, and the blood delivers it. Oxygen is carried by the microscopic, doughnut-shaped red cells. These make up nearly half the blood's volume.

Each red cell contains millions of molecules of the substance haemoglobin, which gives the blood its red colour. In the lungs, haemoglobin attaches itself to molecules of oxygen. It carries them piggy-back fashion to the body cells, where oxygen is more scarce, and releases its load.

If something goes wrong with this system and there

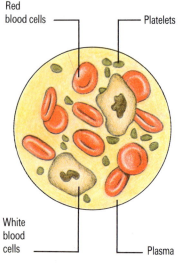

Red blood cells

Platelets

White blood cells

Plasma

Left: Blood under the microscope. About 45 per cent of blood's volume is cells, mostly red, with some platelets and a few white cells. The other 55 per cent is a yellowish fluid called plasma – 90 per cent water and 10 per cent chemicals.

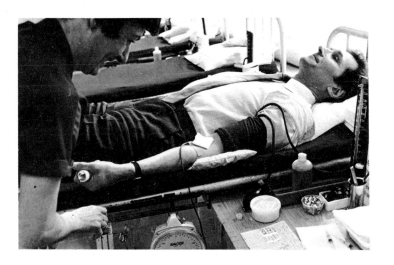

isn't enough healthy hae-moglobin the result is anaemia, where the person becomes pale, listless and breathless.

Blood also collects waste carbon dioxide from the body tissues. Some of the carbon dioxide is carried in red cells, but most of it dissolves in the plasma.

There are five million red cells in a drop of blood. Each cell lives for about four months, carrying oxygen on perhaps 40,000 journeys around the body. It then becomes old and worn out, dies, and its contents are recycled by the liver and spleen. To replace the red cells that die, two million new red cells are made in the bone marrow every second.

Above: Blood donors each give half a litre of blood to help those who are injured or in need of surgery. The donated blood is soon replaced naturally by the donor's body.

The blood's white army

During an infection like mumps, the **glands** in your neck swell and become painful. These glands are lymph glands and, along with the blood, they are part of the body's infection-fighting system. This is based on an army of white blood cells.

There are about 5,000 white cells in a pinprick of blood. Although they are called 'white' cells they are more like transparent jelly.

The various types of white cells have different names,

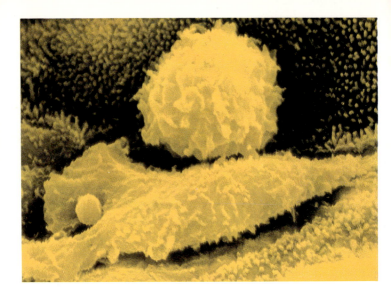

Above: In this scanning electron micrograph a macrophage, a type of white cell, is cleaning the lungs by devouring a small particle.

but they all have one main aim: to fight infections. When **microbes** such as bacteria or viruses invade the body and start to multiply, setting up an infection, the defensive army of white cells goes into action.

Like any good army, the white cells use different tactics. Some, the macrophages, gobble up invading microbes whole. Others, the lymphocytes, make special molecules called antibodies that kill the invaders. Some antibodies work like limpet mines on ships. They stick to the outside of the invader and eventually cause it to burst open.

Some types of white cell multiply and are 'trained' in the lymph gland to go out into the body and attack the invaders. This is why these glands swell during an infection, as massive numbers of cells are sent into battle

Cuts and clots

In addition to red and white cells, the blood contains platelets. These are more like bits of cells than whole cells. When blood comes into contact with air, the platelets become sticky and clump together. This is extremely

useful, because if blood is in contact with air, this means it is leaking through a cut.

In addition, chemicals in the blood fluid link together at the site of the leak, into microscopic ropes and nets made of a substance called fibrin. This traps red cells and more platelets. Gradually the mish-mash of fibrin, red and white cells and platelets hardens to form a clot that seals the wound.

Central heating
Blood acts like water in a central heating system. It absorbs heat from busy, hot organs such as the liver and the working muscles, and takes it to the cooler, less active parts. In this way heat is spread out and the entire body stays at its best working temperature.

Fright, fight and flight
Blood has yet another role: as a distributor of chemically-coded messages in the form of hormones.

Imagine seeing a poisonous snake or hearing a noise in the night. Your heart pounds, you become pale and sweaty, you breathe faster, and you are ready to jump and run at the slightest thing. All this happens because your brain has instructed your adrenal glands to release a hormone, adrenaline, into the blood.

As adrenaline travels round the body it causes various changes, getting the body ready for action. The heart beats faster and the lungs take in more oxygen. More energy-giving sugars flow into the blood. The blood vessels in the skin become narrower (which makes your skin pale) while those to the muscles widen. The muscles, with their extra blood supply, are ready to move the body as it either

Above: In some people the body's infection-fighting system goes wrong. It attacks harmless things like breathed-in pollen grains. The result is the runny nose and sneezing of hay fever.

COLUMBIA PICTURES present

DANA ANDREWS
PEGGY CUMMINS
and NIALL MacGINNIS

Chosen...singled out
to die...victim of
his imagination or
victim of a demon?

Night of the Demon

Screenplay by CHARLES BENNETT and HAL E. CHESTER
Based on the Story "Casting the Runes" by Montague R. James
Directed by JACQUES TOURNEUR · Produced by FRANK BEVIS

Executive Producer HAL E. CHESTER
A SABRE FILM Production

fights the threat or flees to safety. The whole reaction to a fright is called 'fight or flight'. This happens even in situations where we don't need extra muscle power – we can feel equally nervous about exams or interviews. This is probably a left-over reaction from a simpler way of life, when fight or flight was the only reaction needed.

Hormones at work

Adrenaline is only one of the many hormones circulating in the blood. Hormones are made in glands called endocrine glands, and each hormone controls a body process.

Above: Frights on the screen can make you jump – and it's all to do with hormones. Because it is only make-believe, many people quite like being 'scared to death'.

The thyroid and parathyroids in the neck regulate the way cells use energy and the way the body uses the mineral calcium. If the parathyroids become diseased the bones can weaken, because their calcium content falls. The pancreas makes the hormone insulin, which also affects energy use. Lack of insulin causes the disease diabetes.

The ovaries in a girl and the testes in a boy are

involved in growth and re-production (see pages 84–87).

The thymus in the chest is an unusual gland. It is present in children but shrinks away in adults. It is thought to help in the fight against bacteria and viruses.

The master gland
All the hormone-producing glands are themselves controlled by hormones made in the pituitary, a pea-sized endocrine gland just under the brain. This gland also makes yet more hormones to regulate the body's general growth and to control the kidneys.

Naturally, where co-ordination is concerned, the brain is involved. The pituitary is connected to the brain by a stalk of nerves, so that the hormonal system and the nervous system can communicate with each other and run the body efficiently.

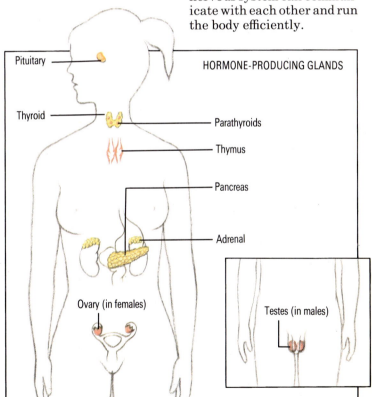

HORMONE-PRODUCING GLANDS

Pituitary

Thyroid

Parathyroids

Thymus

Pancreas

Adrenal

Ovary (in females)

Testes (in males)

You Are What You Eat

The human species has come a long way since prehistoric times. Our ancestors had to forage for food – picking fruits and shoots, gnawing at roots, and hunting wild animals. Finding enough food took a long time. Nowadays it's only too easy to buy precooked meals from the supermarket, or to pop into the take-away for a burger and chips.

Yet there's a problem. Our food may be modern, precooked and pre-packaged, but our digestive system is still designed for a stone-age diet. Evolution works slowly and has not had time to adapt our digestive organs to the new foods that our brains

People who eat a simple diet with lots of vegetables and fruit are eating the kind of foods our bodies are designed for.

have cleverly invented. In recent years doctors have discovered that several diseases – including some heart diseases and cancers – are linked to eating the wrong type of food.

Healthy food
Prehistoric man did not eat salamis, sausages, burgers and other fatty, processed meats which contain a lot of animal fats. He didn't dine on cheese and other dairy produce, or cakes. He didn't eat

lots of sugar, or sweets, chocolate, cakes and biscuits. Too much of these things is bad for us.

What primitive man *did* eat was plenty of **fibre** (roughage) which is found in vegetables, fruit and cereals. He ate meat, but probably only in small quantities. In general, this is still the healthiest diet for our bodies today.

Above: Eating nothing but burgers, chips and cream cakes is unhealthy, though the occasional 'junk' meal does no harm in an otherwise balanced diet.

Break down, build up

Consider the amount of food you have eaten over the last month or so. Some of that pile has become you – your nerves, muscles, blood and skin. Some of it provided energy to drive the body's chemistry and movements. The rest of the food was not used, and passed through the body's waste disposal system.

Food has two main uses: raw materials for growth and repair, and energy. It is the digestive system's job to take whatever you eat, from potatoes to pizzas to pork chops, and break it down physically and chemically into small building-block molecules, and absorb these into the bloodstream.

Thought for food

How does the body know it's dinner time? It is thought that the energy-providing sugars in the blood are gradually used up and their levels fall. The brain detects this and its 'feeding centre' makes us feel hungry. After the meal the stomach is stretched and full, and the brain detects this and orders us to stop eating.

Hunger is not the only reason for eating. You may not feel the least bit hungry, but if someone offers a tempting cake, you would probably not refuse. So we are able to control the amount of food we eat to a certain extent, to keep our bodies slim and healthy.

The beginning of the journey

You pop a piece of food into your mouth, chew it and swallow it. That seems the end of the matter. But for the food it is the start of an epic journey taking a day or more, through eight or nine metres of digestive system.

First stop is the mouth. Teeth chop, chew and grind the food into a mushy lump as the tongue moulds and moves it. Hot food is cooled, cold food is warmed. Three pairs of glands add a watery substance called saliva. You make one to two litres of

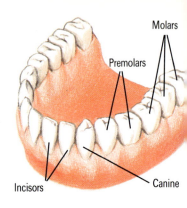

Above: Our 32 teeth (16 in each jaw) have different shapes for different jobs. Incisors cut, canines hold and tear, premolars and molars grind and crush.

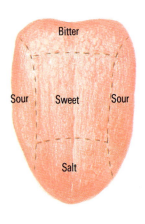

Above: Taste buds detect only four basic tastes, each on a different part of the tongue. Most flavours we experience are combinations of the four basic ones.

saliva each day, to lubricate your food and also to start the first of many chemical attacks on it. Saliva contains an **enzyme** called ptyalin that attacks starch in the food.

Choppers and grinders

Some foods, like nuts and gristle, are quite hard, so teeth must be even harder in order to break them down. The tough whitish covering of a tooth is called enamel and it is the hardest substance in the body. It has no nerves and feels no pain.

Under the enamel is a softer, porous material called dentine. In the middle

74

of the tooth is the pulp, a mixture of nerves and blood vessels.

Dirty teeth are covered with bacteria. As they feed on sugar in the food, the bacteria make acid as a by-product. The acid softens the enamel and gradually eats away a hole. Hot or cold or strongly-flavoured foods can now reach the dentine and pass through to the sensitive pulp. We all know the result: toothache. To prevent this process, dental decay, you need to remove the bacteria by regular toothbrushing and starve them by eating as little sugar as possible.

Smelling tastes

When the nose is blocked by a cold, food seems to have little taste. In fact, it is because the food has little smell. The taste buds on the tongue, which taste four basic sensations, are not affected by a nasal cold. But smelling cells in the nose, which pick up more than 300 different odours, are affected by a cold. When we eat, the smell of the food wafts backwards from the rear of the mouth up into the nose. The brain combines smells and tastes to give the flavour of food. A blocked nose stops us from smelling the food, which means poor 'taste'.

Below: Visit the dentist at least once a year. The dentist can help by removing tooth decay, but it's up to you to clean your teeth after meals.

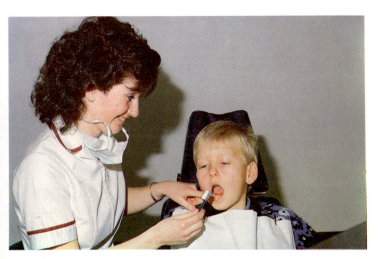

Journey to the Stomach

When we swallow food we usually think of it as going 'into' the body. In fact this is not so. The digestive tube or 'tract' forms a long tunnel running through the body, and so food in the tract is technically not inside the body. Only when it is absorbed through the wall of the tract does it enter body tissues.

Moving your meal

The whole digestive tube, from mouth to anus, has muscular walls that rhythmically squeeze food on its way by waves of contraction called **peristalsis**. The front and back ends of the tube are under the brain's conscious control: we can choose when to swallow, and when to release faeces (undigested food). But the rest of the muscles of the tract work automatically, without us thinking about it. Even when we are asleep the digestive tract muscles are working, steadily pushing food on its journey.

Swallowing

To start swallowing, the tongue pushes a lump of food to the back of the mouth.

Then two trapdoors close. One, the palate (a flap of fleshy tissue at the back of the roof of the mouth) shuts off the route up into the nose. If you breathe in through your nose and then try to swallow, your breathing suddenly stops as this trapdoor closes. The second trapdoor, the epiglottis, closes off the top of the windpipe so that food does not go that way and choke us.

The only remaining route is down the oesophagus, or gullet. This is a muscular tube 25 centimetres long that squeezes food or drink down through the chest, past the heart and lungs to the stomach.

The stomach

When we have a pain somewhere around the navel (belly-button), we usually think of it as 'stomach ache'. In fact the stomach is much higher than this – it is just below and to the left of the breast bone, behind the lower ribs. Pains lower down are more likely to come from the small intestine, which is coiled into loops in the area behind the navel. Butterflies and other feelings 'in the pit

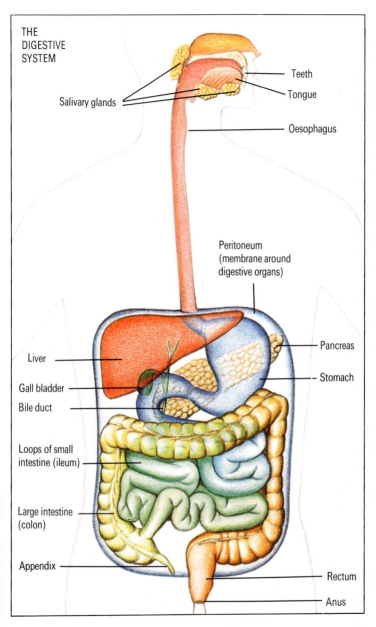

THE DIGESTIVE SYSTEM

Salivary glands

Teeth

Tongue

Oesophagus

Peritoneum (membrane around digestive organs)

Pancreas

Liver

Stomach

Gall bladder

Bile duct

Loops of small intestine (ileum)

Large intestine (colon)

Appendix

Rectum

Anus

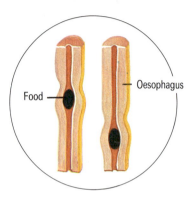

Food is pushed along the digestive tract by waves of contraction of the muscles in its wall. This means someone can swallow even if upside down.

Food — —Oesophagus

of the stomach' also usually come from the small intestine as it squirms and squeezes in response to nervousness or fright.

The acid bath

The stomach makes an acid which attacks the food. The acid is excellent for killing bacteria in the food so that they cannot cause a stomach infection. It also atacks food chemically, dissolving the chewed-up lumps into a semi-liquid pulp.

But what stops the acid burning a hole in the stomach? The answer is that cells in the stomach wall make a thick mucus that lines the wall and keeps the

acid at bay. Other stomach cells make protein-digesting enzymes to attack the food. The protective mucus barrier keeps out these enzymes as well.

In a few people, the stomach makes too much acid or not enough mucus. The acid erodes a painful spot in the stomach or in the next part of the tract, the duodenum (the first section of the small intestine). The raw spot is a peptic ulcer.

The full stomach's muscular wall contracts regularly every 20 seconds or so, to squash and churn up the contents and send them into the next portion of the tube – the intestine. After a big meal the stomach may hold one or even two litres of food and fluid, and take five hours to empty.

An absorbing business

After the stomach comes the small intestine. This makes several enzymes that continue the chemical digestion of food. It is also the main site for absorbing nutrients. They pass through its thin lining into the rich blood supply flowing through its wall.

To absorb as much as possible the small intestine has several special design features. First, it is very long – five or six metres, coiled inside the body. Second, it has tiny 'fingers' sticking from its lining, rather like a soft-pile carpet. Each finger, or villus, is up to one millimetre long and there are 20 or 30 to a square millimetre. Together the coiling and the fingers give the small intestine's lining an area of nearly 20 square metres. This is over ten times the skin's area, and enough to absorb everything you need (except oxygen) to stay alive.

The villi in the small intestine (shown highly magnified) contain blood and lymph vessels which take up and carry away the digested food.

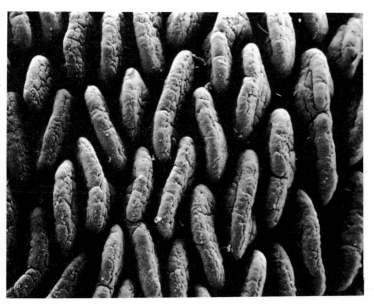

Fibre in food

The undigestible parts of the food are squeezed into the large intestine, an upside-down U-shaped tube one and a half metres long and six centimetres in diameter. Here some of the water is absorbed back into the body.

The large intestine, or large bowel, works best if it has a lot of bulk to grip on. Fibre in food is mostly undigested and provides this bulk. People who eat too little fibre have small, dry, hard-to-pass faeces and they are more at risk from constipation and bowel disease. Fibre keeps the water content of the faeces high, so that they are easy to pass.

An end to the matter

Finally, the faeces are stored in the rectum, the last portion of the tract before its outlet, the anus. Faeces contain undigested remains of food, plus rubbed-off bits of intestinal lining from the long journey through the tract, and also millions of bacteria. These bacteria are 'friendly', living in the intestines and helping to digest some of the substances our own enzymes can't deal with. In return we provide the bacteria with a good supply of nutrients.

Food processing

Absorbing nutrients into the blood is only half the battle.

Left: Even a modern chemical refinery is put to shame by the liver. This organ is involved in over 500 chemical processes in the body.

Below: These organs make food-digesting chemicals or change the composition of the blood.

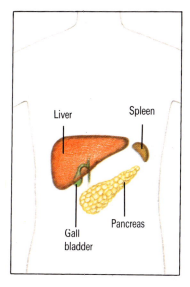

Liver   Spleen

Gall
bladder   Pancreas

Nutrients come in all shapes and sizes and they require further alteration and refining before body cells can use them.

Our own chemical refinery is the liver. It is our largest gland, weighing one and a half kilograms, and it plays a central role in hundreds of chemical processes in the body. It makes enzymes, adjusts the amount of energy-giving sugar in the blood, and stores vitamins. It detoxifies (makes harmless) substances like alcohol that would otherwise poison the body. Too much alcohol strains and damages the liver, causing the disease cirrhosis.

Just below the liver is a small bag called the gall bladder. It stores a fluid, bile, which is made by the liver and released into the intestine as food passes through. Bile helps to digest the fatty parts of food.

Also under the liver is the pancreas. This gland manufactures a litre of powerful enzyme-containing digestive juices each day and empties them along a thin tube into the small intestine. Pancreatic juices are alkaline and help to neutralize the acid from the stomach.

Near the pancreas is the spleen. This helps the liver to 'clean' the blood by breaking down old red cells and removing bacteria. It also stores red cells. During exercise, when more red cells are needed, the spleen contracts to squeeze its stores into the circulation. You may feel this as a pain called a 'stitch' in your side.

Waste Disposal

The body is nearly two-thirds water, and this must be kept clean by the disposal of wastes and poisons. There also has to be a balance between water coming in (as food and drink) and water going out. To do these jobs the body has two sophisticated filters – the kidneys.

The renal artery leading to each kidney is very wide. The equivalent of the body's entire blood volume passes through each kidney once every five minutes or so. The blood flows into tiny capillaries that branch and lead to more than a million microscopic filters, which are called glomeruli. Each day 200 litres of water, containing salts and other chemicals, pass through the glomeruli, out of the blood. But nearly all the water and some of the useful chemicals, like glucose, are reabsorbed back into the blood. This leaves only a litre or so of water containing concentrated wastes: urine.

Below: The racing cyclist has no time to stop – but he must make time to drink. He loses over a litre of water each hour through sweat, as well as losing water in breathed-out air and urine formation.

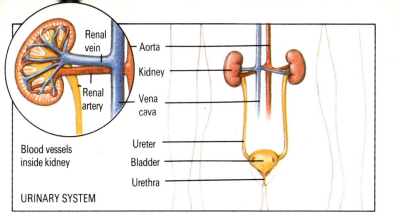

Blood vessels
inside kidney

Renal
vein

Renal
artery

Aorta

Kidney

Vena
cava

Ureter

Bladder

Urethra

URINARY SYSTEM

A balancing act

If you are out in the hot sun all day, sweating but with nothing to drink, your body needs to conserve water. In cold conditions you do not sweat but you may take lots of hot drinks, so your body must remove excess water. The amounts of various salts in the body need to be kept constant, too, so that cells are able to continue their chemical reactions.

The kidneys do this balancing act by altering the amounts of water and salts in blood. If there is too much water, they filter some away as urine. If there is too much salt, they filter that away too. The kidneys' instructions come in the form of hormones from the brain and from the adrenal glands, which are positioned on top of each kidney.

Above: The kidneys are tucked under the ribs. Each kidney is about 11 cms high and 6 cms wide, and weighs around 140 grams. The ureters, which carry urine to the bladder, are each 30 cms long and 3 mms in diameter.

Urine drips steadily from each kidney down a long tube, the ureter, to the bladder. This stretchy, muscle-walled bag is the size and shape of a prune when empty, but it slowly fills to hold about half a litre of fluid. Another tube, the urethra, connects the bladder to the outside.

Well before the bladder is full, sensors in its wall detect the amount it is being stretched and send signals to the brain. Although we can put it off for a certain amount of time, in the end we have to empty the bladder.

83

A New Life

Any complicated machine, from a car engine to an oil rig, is built from a set of plans or blueprints. The human machine is no exception. Its blueprints are in the form of a chemical called **DNA** (deoxyribonucleic acid). It is DNA which helps to decide what we look like, how we grow, and even influences how we behave.

Just as letters combine to make words, and words make sentences, so the chemical units of DNA form the long lists of chemically-coded sentences termed **genes**. These contain all the information needed to build and run a human body.

DNA molecules are in almost every type of body cell, packaged as microscopic threads named **chromosomes**. There are 46 chromosomes, as 23 pairs, in each cell. Cells in the body are continually dividing in order to replace old, worn out cells. Every time a cell divides all 46 chromosomes are copied so that the two new cells each have a full set.

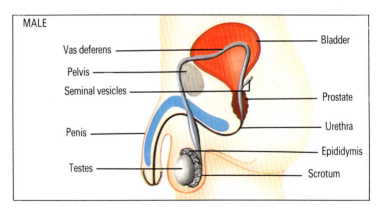

MALE

Vas deferens

Pelvis

Seminal vesicles

Penis

Testes

Bladder

Prostate

Urethra

Epididymis

Scrotum

A man's sperm cells are made in his two testes and stored in the epididymis, a long coiled tube. During sexual intercourse the sperm travel along another tube, the vas deferens. Fluids are added to them by small glands called the seminal vesicles and prostate. Then they pass along the urethra and out of the end of the penis.

A new human being starts life as one cell. This is made by a sperm cell from the father joining with, or fertilizing, an egg cell produced by the mother.

If sperm and egg each contained 46 chromosomes then the fertilized egg, and so every cell in the baby's body, would contain 92 chromosomes. In the next generation, each cell would have 184 chromosomes. To stop this doubling the sperm and the egg cells contain only a half-set of chromosomes, one of each of the 23 pairs. When the sperm and egg join, the fertilized egg is back to the normal 46.

Getting together

Sperm are made in a man's testes. They are tadpole-like cells each about one-twentieth of a millimetre long. A man makes many millions of new sperm every day.

Egg cells are made in a woman's ovaries while she is still a baby in her mother's womb. When she is an adult she has about 300,000 eggs, each one-tenth of a millimetre in diameter. Once a month, one egg ripens and leaves the ovary in a process known as ovulation. The egg travels down the oviduct (egg tube) towards the womb.

During sexual intercourse the man places his penis in

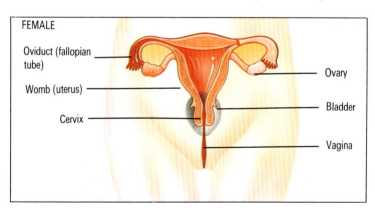

FEMALE

Oviduct (fallopian tube)

Womb (uterus)

Cervix

Ovary

Bladder

Vagina

The woman's egg cells are stored in the two ovaries. Each month one egg ripens under control of a hormone, and leaves the ovary to enter the funnel-shaped end of the oviduct. **It is wafted along by tiny hairs lining the oviduct, to the womb. On its way, if it meets a sperm it will be fertilized, and a new life will begin.**

the vagina of the woman and releases up to 300 million sperm in four millilitres of fluid (called semen). The sperm swim into the woman's womb and along the oviducts. If an egg happens to be coming the other way, one sperm will fertilize the egg and a new life begins.

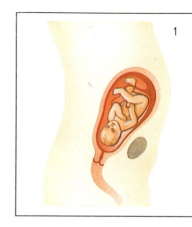

The developing baby

The fertilized egg floats down the oviduct to the womb. It divides every few hours, making two cells, then four, then eight, and so on. When it reaches the womb, about five days after fertilization, it has become a

Below: The tiny tadpole-like sperm cells swim to join with the egg cell to fertilize it. This will then make a barrier around itself to prevent more sperm from joining.

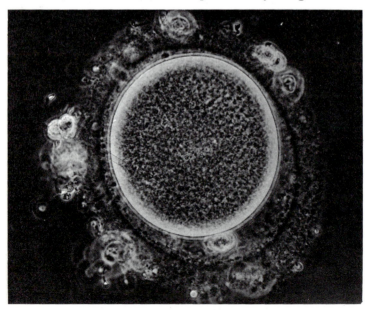

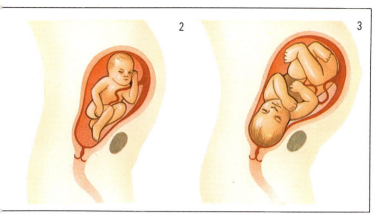

2 3

tiny ball of more than one hundred cells.

The ball of cells eats its way into the womb lining and feeds on the mother's blood and tissue fluids. The cells continue to divide. At first they are all the same, but gradually they become nerve cells, muscle cells, blood cells and so on, as they form the developing organs.

Five weeks after fertilization the baby is less than ten millimetres long but it has a brain, a beating heart and the beginnings of a face, arms and legs. Two months after fertilization it is still only 25 millimetres long, yet it is unmistakably a tiny human being with all its major organs formed. Over the next seven months it grows to 500 millimetres long and 3,500 grams in weight.

Above: Three stages during pregnancy, showing the growing baby: (1) 18 weeks after fertilization; (2) 26 weeks (3) 32 weeks after fertilization.

By the time it is born, nine months after fertilization, the baby is fully formed – but its life is just beginning.

Birth day
When the baby is ready to be born the mother's pituitary gland releases a hormone, which stimulates powerful contractions of the muscle in the wall of the womb. This is one of the strongest muscles in the body. The exit from the womb, the cervix, slowly widens. At last, after several hours of effort, the baby is pushed out of the womb, along the vagina and into the outside world.

Growing Up

New babies are virtually helpless apart from a few instinctive, built-in reactions such as coughing, sucking and swallowing. Yet within a year they may be walking and saying one or two simple words. By the time they go to school they probably know several hundred words and the basic rules of grammar, can ride a bicycle and draw recognizable pictures. While their bodies are growing, their brains are also developing at an amazing rate.

Child to adult

During the early school years body growth is steady. The average child gains five centimetres in height and two and a half kilograms in weight each year. Then suddenly, from the age of about 11 in girls and 13 in boys, the body changes rapidly. This is the time we call puberty.

A girl's height increases rapidly. Her breasts swell, her hips become rounded, and hair grows between her

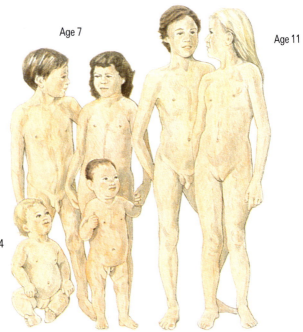

Age 7

Age 11

Age 4

88

legs. Inside, her ovaries start to release one egg each month. This is accompanied by thickening of the womb lining to nourish the egg if it is fertilized. If not, the egg and womb lining are lost from the body as the monthly menstruation (a 'period').

A boy also gains height rapidly. His muscles develop and hair grows on his face, chest, armpits and between his legs. His penis and testes enlarge and the testes begin to make sperm.

By the time the girl is about 14 and the boy is 15, they are physically able to have children.

Although the body is grown up, the mind still has some way to go. Over the years it matures and develops these qualities we pride ourselves on – intelligence, understanding, wisdom and tolerance. Only then are we mature human beings.

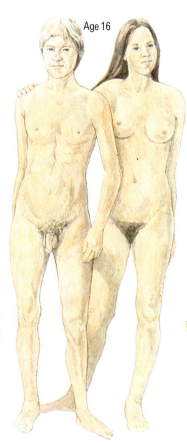

Age 16

Below: On the whole, the human body is not that different from other members of the animal world. What sets us apart is our intelligence and ability to learn – especially about ourselves.

Glossary

Alveoli Microscopic air-filled bubbles in the lungs where oxygen is absorbed into the body and carbon dioxide is released into the air.

Axon The long, wire-like part of a nerve cell that carries messages to other cells.

Capillary The smallest blood vessel with a wall only one cell thick.

Cartilage The smooth, tough substance that covers the ends of bones in a joint.

Cell The basic 'building block' of all living things. An amoeba is one cell; a human is 50 million million cells.

Centre In the brain, an area dealing with nerve messages going to and from one part of the body, such as the eye.

Cerebral cortex The surface layer of the cerebral hemispheres, the main part of the brain.

Chromosomes Thread-like structures inside cells which contain DNA.

Cochlea The pea-sized organ in the ear which turns sound waves into nerve messages.

Cone A light-detecting cell in the eye that sees in colour and picks out fine detail.

Coronary To do with the blood vessels that supply the heart muscle.

Dendrite The short, wire-like parts of a nerve cell that receive messages from other cells.

Dermis The thick under-layer of the skin, beneath the epidermis.

DNA De-oxyribonucleic acid, the 'chemical of life' found in every cell. It contains chemically-coded instructions on how to build and run the body.

Enzyme A chemical that speeds up or slows down a chemical reaction in a living thing.

Epidermis The thin, mostly dead outer layer of the skin.

Fibre A substance found in some plant foods, which is not digestible but gives 'bulk' to out diet and helps to keep our digestive system healthy.

Genes Instructions, in the form of DNA, for building and running the body.

Gland An organ that makes a certain chemical for the body, such as a hormone; also, an organ that contains certain cells which fight disease.

Habituation When a cell or animal 'gets used to' something and no longer reacts to it.

Hormone A 'chemical messenger' made in a gland, which travels in the blood and affects certain parts of the body.

Keratin A tough, stringy substance found in skin, hair and nails.

Kinaesthetic The sense by which we 'feel' the positions of our various body parts.

Ligaments Strong strap-like structures that hold bones together in a joint.

Marrow The jelly-like substance inside some bones, which makes blood cells.

Melanin A dark-brown chemical in skin and hair, which gives them their colour.

Microbe A microscopic living thing such as a bacterium or a virus. Some microbes cause diseases.

Motor Carrying nerve messages from brain to muscles.

Motor area The part of the brain which controls body movements.

Neurone A nerve cell, specialized to carry electrical nerve messages.

Organ Various tissues collected together to do one task, such as the heart which pumps blood.

Peristalsis Waves of muscle contraction which push material along a tube, such as in the digestive system.

Pigments Coloured chemicals found in the skin, eyes and other body parts.

Plasma The liquid part of blood, without the cells.

Pulmonary To do with the lungs. Pulmonary arteries carry blood to the lungs.

Reflex An automatic reaction by the body, for example, the eye pupil becoming smaller in bright light.

Retina The layer of light-detecting cells in the eye.

Rod A light-detecting cell in the eye that sees only in black-and-white.

Sensors A cell or organ specialized to detect something, such as light or sound, and turn it into nerve messages.

Sensory Carrying nerve messages from the sensors to the brain.

Synapse The tiny gap between one nerve cell and another, which a nerve message crosses in chemical form.

System Various organs working together to do one major task inside the body, such as circulating blood.

Tendon The strong, tapering end of a muscle which joins it to a bone.

Tissue A collection of cells of one type, such as nerve cells or muscle cells.

Visual pigments Coloured light-detecting chemicals in the rods and cones of the eye.

Index

Page numbers in *italics* refer to illustrations.

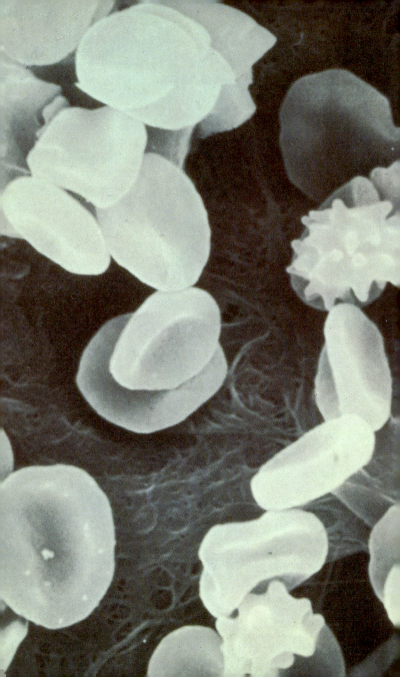

Acknowledgements

Endpapers Gene Cox, Page 6 Lucas Film, 10 Zefa, 18 Zefa, 21 Multimedia, 26 Harold Harris/Zefa, 27 British Museum of Natural History, 33 Colorsport, 31 Sally Anne Thompson, 34 Blind Institute, 36 Institute of Trichologists, 39 Zefa, 40 Colorsport, 44 Middlesex Hospital, 48 Cynthia Clarke, 50 Zefa, 52–53 Zefa, 55 Robert Harding, 57 Health Education Council, 61 Mary Evans, 65 Gene Cox, 67 National Blood Transfusion Service/Rex Features, 68 Science Photo Library, 69 Zefa, 70 National Film Archive, 75 Dept of Dental Illustration, Glasgow Dental Hospital & School, 78 Zefa, 79 John Watney, 80 Zefa, 86 M.R.C. Reproductive Biology Unit Centre.

Picture Research by Penny J. Warn & Jackie Cookson.